Red Activists and Black Freedom

This book deals with the forgotten history of the civil rights movement. The American Left played a significant part in the origins of that movement, whose history has traditionally been focused on the later 1940's and early 1950's. This approach needs serious re-thinking in light of what took place in the later 1930's with the organization and activity of groups like the Southern Negro Youth Congress that brought both African-American and white workers and students together in the fight for economic and social justice. Thanks to the post-World War II Red Scare such groups as well as Left African-American leaders like Esther and James Jackson have been overlooked or excised from an exciting, controversial, and important story. With all due credit to the churches which played such a pivotal role in finally winning Blacks their civil rights, the early history involving the Left, workers of both races, and the labor unions must be assimilated into America's memory, for there were important continuities between what they did and the later church-based struggle.

This book was published as a special issue of *American Communist History*.

David Levering Lewis is a Pulitzer Prize winning historian who is Julius Silver University Professor at New York University.

Michael H. Nash has been Director of the Tamiment Library and Robert F. Wagner Labor Archives at New York University since 2002. He holds a PhD in American History from SUNY Binghamton, and has served as Chief Curator, Library Collections at the Hagley Museum and Library (Wilmington, DE).

Daniel J. Leab is Professor of History at Seton Hall University, and founding editor of *American Communist History*. His most recent book is *Orwell Subverted: the CIA and the filming of Animal Farm* (2007).

Red Activists and Black Freedom

James and Esther Jackson and the
Long Civil Rights Revolution

Edited by David Levering Lewis,
Michael H. Nash and Daniel J. Leab

Routledge
Taylor & Francis Group
LONDON AND NEW YORK

First published 2010 by Routledge
2 Park Square, Milton Park, Abingdon, Oxon, OX14 4RN

Simultaneously published in the USA and Canada
by Routledge
270 Madison Avenue, New York, NY 10016

Routledge is an imprint of the Taylor & Francis Group, an informa business

Typeset in Plantin by Value Chain, India
Printed and bound in Great Britain by TJI Digital, Padstow, Cornwall

British Library Cataloguing in Publication Data
A catalogue record for this book is available from the British Library

ISBN10: 0-415-47255-5
ISBN13: 978-0-415-47255-5

Contents

Notes on Contributors   vii

Preface   ix
Daniel J. Leab

Foreword   xv
Michael H. Nash

Introduction   1
David Levering Lewis

1. The Jacksons   5
    Robin D. G. Kelley

2. James and Esther Jackson: A Historical Assessment   11
    David Levering Lewis

3. Fundamentally Determined: James E. Jackson and Esther Cooper
    Jackson and the Southern Negro Youth Congress – 1937–1946   21
    Johnetta Richards

4. Esther V. Cooper's "The Negro Woman Domestic Worker in Relation to
    Trade Unionism": Black Left Feminism and the Popular Front   33
    Erik S. McDuffie

5. "All those rosy dreams we cherish": James Jackson and Esther Cooper's
    Marriage on the Front Lines of the Double Victory Campaign   41
    Sara E. Rzeszutek

6. FREEDOMWAYS   57
    Michael Nash and Daniel J. Leab

7. James and Esther Jackson: A Personal Perspective   69
    Maurice Jackson

8. "Death for Negro lynching!" The Communist Party, USA's Position
    on the African American Question   73
    Timothy Johnson

9. Civil Rights Unionism and the Black Freedom Struggle   85
    Robert Korstad

10. Lorraine Hansberry's Freedom Family   89
    Michael Anderson

11. James and Esther Jackson: Connecting the Past to the Present 101
    Angela Davis

    Index   107

Notes on Contributors

Michael Anderson is a former editor at the *New York Times*. He is completing a biography of Lorraine Hansberry.

Angela Davis is Professor Emeritus at the University of California at Santa Cruz. She is the author of *Blues Legacies and Black Feminism*.

Erik S. McDuffie is an Assistant Professor in Africana Studies and in the Gender and Women Studies Program at the University of Illinois at Urbana. His book *"Toward a Brighter Dawn: Black Women and American Communism, 1930–1956"* is forthcoming.

Maurice Jackson is an Assistant Professor in the Department of History at Georgetown University, and is the author of *"Let this Voice be Heard: Anthony Benezet and Atlantic Abolition"*.

Timothy Johnson is the Africana Studies Librarian at New York University.

Robin D. G. Kelley is Professor of American Studies and Ethnicity at the University of Southern California. His most recent book is *Freedom Dreams: The Black Radical Imagination*. Professor Kelley is also the author of *Race Rebels: Culture, Politics, and the Black Working Class*.

Robert Korstad is an Associate Professor of Public Policy and History at Duke University. His publications include *Civil Rights Unionism: Tobacco Workers and the Struggle for Democracy in the Mid-Twentieth Century South*.

Daniel J. Leab is a Professor of History at Seton Hall University and editor of *American Communist History*. His most recent book is *Orwell Subverted: the CIA and the Filming of Animal Farm*, Penn State Press, 2008.

David Levering Lewis is the Julius Silver Professor of History at New York University. The first volume of his Du Bois biography *W.E.B. Du Bois: Biography of a Race, 1868-1919* won the Bancroft and Pulitzer prizes. Volume 2 *W.E.B. Du Bois: The Fight for Equality and the American Century, 1919-1963* won the Pulitzer Prize for biography.

Michael H. Nash is the Director of the Tamiment Library at New York University. His publications include *Conflict and Accommodation: Coal Miners, Steel Workers, and Socialism*.

Johnetta Richards is an Associate Professor of Africana Studies at San Francisco State University. Her essay in this volume draws on her doctoral dissertation "The Southern Negro Youth Congress: A History, 1937–1949".

Sara E. Rzeszutek received her Ph.D. in U.S. and African American History from Rutgers University. Her dissertation "Love and Activism: James and Esther Cooper Jackson and the Black Freedom Movement in the United States, 1914–1968" focuses on the intersection between personal and political life during the Black Freedom Movement and the Cold War.

Preface

DANIEL J. LEAB

There is no need to justify publication of these essays dealing with Esther and James Jackson, and their involvement and that of other Communists in the run-up to the Second Reconstruction. They all deserve to be remembered for their gallant often lonely battles against the racism and economic inequities which pervaded the United States during the heyday of their activities. What they and their allies accomplished as well as their influence and impact should not be forgotten. Their chosen vehicles, the Communist Party of the USA (CPUSA) and its allied organizations, reflect the Party's high-profile campaign on behalf of the exploited of all colors.

Certainly for many of these years, indeed from the onset of the Depression in 1929 to the period immediately after the end of World War II the Communists and their allies were the most outspoken challengers of the racist status quo, especially in the Deep South. Because of their policy of mass protests and the noise surrounding them (drowning out less public and much less dramatic legal maneuvers, sometimes characterized as "armchair activism") African-Americans knew about the efforts of the Reds to aid Black people.[1]

The emphasis of these essays on the efforts of the CPUSA, and on the role of individual Communists in these battles as well as the resulting legacies, does require elucidation because the relationship between the CP and African-Americans has been the subject of considerable, often contradictory, and sometimes bitter historical controversy. The historian Charles Martin over two decades ago pointed out that for some time historians generally treated Communist efforts to aid African Americans to achieve their political and social

---

[1] Charles H. Martin, *The Angelo Herndon Case and Southern Justice* (Baton Rouge, LA: Louisiana State University Press, 1976), 19.

rights "as nothing more than crude, cynical attempts to exploit Blacks for propaganda purposes without actually securing anything tangible for them." He also noted that starting in the 1970s writers of history have "suggested that the situation was more complex than previously depicted and that Communists did ... produce results."[2]

This collection of essays eschews the more traditional response to the relationship between African-Americans and the efforts of the CPUSA as an organization and of individual Communists. Nor does this collection of essays attempt to establish a new synthesis. Written by both scholars and activists these essays are one side of a historical equation and celebrate the Jacksons, active members of the Party, as well as the efforts of other Communists who campaigned aggressively for social, political, and economic justice for Black people at a time when African-Americans faced barriers that seemed insurmountable. In effect this collection of essays is a commentary on the relations between African-Americans and the Communists from a particular point of view and should be regarded as such.

There is nothing even-handed about these essays and their authors' approach, and there was nothing even-handed about the despairing lives of most African-Americans that necessitated a struggle that culminated in the modern civil rights movement. These essays present forcefully and cogently a challenge to the traditional historiography. It should be remembered, more-over, that the Jacksons joined the Party after it abandoned the sectarian Third Period (1929–1935) policies which led Communists to scorn joint ventures even in mass protest efforts such as the Scottsboro case.

Think back to what life was like for the average African-American in the U.S. during the decade in which the Jacksons grew to maturity. Think about how the world must have looked to these intelligent, perceptive, ambitious young people. The Scottsboro case was still a very live issue and symbolized the twisted "justice" which African-Americans might expect from the established legal system (nine Black adolescents, aged 12, 13, and 17 were falsely charged with rape; all but one was given a death sentence; ultimately, thanks especially to the exertions of the International Labor Defense, an organization known to be Communist dominated, the defendants were spared execution; but the case which began in the early 1930s raged on for years; not until the "boys" were men did their unjust incarceration cease).

And it was not just such perversions of the legal system which Blacks faced in a South, poisoned by racism. At the time the Jacksons began their activities there, Black people were denied the vote through a variety of means including literacy tests, the poll tax, and outright extra-legal intimidation. African-Americans were denied access to most public facilities, private clubs, and white eating places. Everywhere there were white and "colored" drinking fountains. Discrimination was not only legal and social, but of course economic as well. Black workers were ruthlessly exploited and their pay was minimal.

---

[2] Martin, p. 13.

African-Americans in the South lived in the United States, but not as an integral part of it.

The rest of the country was not without racial barriers. Even liberal New York City had its limitations for African-Americans. When a well-to-do Black family relocated to the Riverdale section of the Bronx, it woke up one morning soon after the move to find signs on the front lawn that read "NIGGER. MOVE OR ELSE!" The noted Black entertainer Cab Calloway, discussing the realities of discrimination at the end of the 1930s, recalled even for the more important Black performers such as himself, New York City had its race barriers—although "anywhere South and West of New York was just hell."[3]

The Jacksons were at the forefront of the fight against such conditions. They found in the CPUSA stalwart comrades and good friends, but as Party members in their efforts they faced a double handicap: the stigma of being Black and Red. The sometimes fierce, many times extra-legal anti-Communism, often stymied Party members in pursuit of its goals and resulted in both physical and legal jeopardy; the South's unrelenting racism which was bolstered by the law could be physically threatening. In 1947 the Jacksons were forced to leave the South. At that time James Jackson, working out of New Orleans, had been targeted for assassination by the Ku Klux Klan and Esther Jackson was being shadowed by the racist Birmingham, Alabama police chief "Bull" Connor and understandably there were fears about her safety.

My co-editors David Levering Lewis and Michael Nash, the initiators of this project, as well as the various individuals who have contributed to this memoir of the Jacksons spell out in detail the physical and legal threats they faced and their unstinting effort (and that of other politically like-minded people) to improve the lives of Black people.

Admittedly, the Jacksons had only limited success before moving to Detroit in 1947. Prejudice is not only extremely tenacious but also can be very dangerous. They were defeated but they were not crushed. Their ideas outlived their failures. They influenced the course of many a future protest. They stimulated organization and individuals. They furthered the spread of militancy. That the Jacksons were committed Communists should not detract from the intelligent nobility of their efforts. Over a very long span of years and despite the legal, political, and ideological vicissitudes the Party faced they remained members in good standing in the CPUSA, he often in a leadership position, notwithstanding all the twists and turns taken by the Party line.

Black people in the long run may have benefited from the efforts of the CP rank and file, but all too often the leadership's notions about what could be done and what should be done were limited and quite unrealistic. James Jackson certainly was not that. He continued to believe "black and white, unite and fight" but not in revolution against all odds. Harry Haywood—a well known Black CP leader and outspoken activist who was expelled from the

---

[3] Calloway quoted in Thomas R. Hietala, *The Fight of the Century: Jack Johnson, Joe Louis, and the Struggle for Racial Equality* (Armonk, NY, London, UK: M.E. Sharpe, Inc., 2001), 207.

Party in 1959 because he opposed its efforts to ally with mainstream civil rights movement—felt that there was a campaign "... to drive militant Blacks out of the Party." He criticized James Jackson for supporting integration rather than a Black nationalist agenda.[4]

The issue of whether the Jacksons were hardliners, as some of their critics have maintained, seems to me extraneous to these essays. Obviously Communism and the Party line informed some, if not many of their actions. But from whatever perspective one views their politics they worked hard to raise the standard of living for Black people, to make their future more secure, to create a better world for them (and for all needy people). It seems to me that they worked diligently at these tasks, did the best they knew how, and deserve credit for what they did manage to achieve. Unlike many of those dedicated to improving humanity in the abstract, the Jacksons were often more practical in their approach, as evidenced, for example, by the Southern Negro Youth Congress (SNYC).

The response to it speaks volumes about changing attitudes toward the relationship between the CP and Blacks—an important aspect of these essays. In 1944 what might then be called the "Negro establishment" found racial militancy "dangerous for interracial peace." The massive race relations project which became known as *An American Dilemma*, paid little attention to the organization despite noting its promising start and positive qualities. Headed by the Swedish economist Gunnar Myrdal, this project utilized both Black and White social scientists. One of them, the African-American Ralph Bunche (a well-regarded social scientist before he became a noted UN civil servant) employed Jackson for some months as one of his three field assistants and commended him for his efforts.

A similar view emerged during the Second Reconstruction. Already, over 40 years ago, The *American Negro Reference Book* asserted that SYNC did develop "approaches and techniques that were to be most valuable ...." Black historian John Hope Franklin also concluded that its campaign against "all forms of segregation" showed clearly a consistent determination "to eradicate all practices that implied ... racial inferiority." A subsequent book on the "Generation Before the Civil Rights Movement in the South" also referred to SNYC's effectiveness in the face of brutal Red-baiting and to its nurturing "leadership qualities in dozens of young Blacks ... ." More recently, so too did a study of the struggle for racial justice in the Cold War South, arguing that although SNYC

---

[4] Harry Haywood, *Black Bolshevik: Autobiography of an Afro-American Communist* (Chicago: Liberator Press, 1978), 618.

[5] Gunnar Myrdal, with the Assistance of Richard Sterner and Arnold Rose, *An American Dilemma: The Negro Problem and Modern Democracy*, 20th Anniversary Edition (New York. Evanston, IL, and London, UK: Harper & Row, 1962 (1944)), 818–819. Jackson had been a "field assistant" to Bunche, one of several, in his putting together a lengthy survey on the "Political Status of the Negro." Jackson, in looking into Boss Crump's machine in Memphis, Bunche recalled, had gotten "notes for a good memorandum" but got into "difficulty" with some members of the machine because of his reporting and had "to leave town" (Bunche quoted in Charles P. Henry, *Ralph Bunche: Model Hero or American Other* (New York and London: New York University Press, 1999), 97).

faced serious obstacles, it "nurtured" and "prepared a generation of young activists for confronting racial barriers."[6]

The efforts by the Jacksons and their allies to remove a fear of tomorrow from African-American life may not as these essays unfortunately indicate have eliminated the many handicaps, both de jure and by custom, Blacks faced. But thanks to the Jacksons (and others like them) these unjust and demeaning barriers became well-known, underwent attack, and proved vulnerable. A fruition of these efforts did not come until the later 1950s and the 1960s with the "Modern Civil Rights Movement" which substantially improved the situation of Black people in the US (but unfortunately did not resolve all the unfair handicaps faced by Americans of all colors).

Blacks became an urban proletariat after World War II as a result of demographic and economic changes caused by the war. As the CP Black activist Hosea Hudson later succinctly put it: "Them houses is grown up, them plantations is briar patches ..., and the Negroes is all in towns." The venue may have changed but the Jacksons maintained their commitment to furthering social justice. James Jackson remained active with the Communist Party and supported the radical movements that sprang up. In the last third of the 20th century, largely outside the Party, Esther Jackson fought for civil rights as well as gender equality, and was the guiding light for the notable radical journal *Freedomways*. Both remained indefatigable in their commitment.[7]

In the early 1950s the fight for civil rights in the South was initially the product of middle class leaders such as Martin Luther King Jr., and officers of local NAACP chapters. Often without acknowledging their debts to people like the Jacksons these Civil Rights leaders built on the ideas and efforts of those who earlier had fought the good fight. In a somewhat different context, politician and government civil servant Rex Tugwell commenting on some forgotten New Dealers asserts that such fighters for social justice should not be overlooked even if their programs did not initially succeed because they "aspired greatly, and we ought to find out all we can about such people. They make a vast difference in our lives." This collection of essays celebrates two individuals who did aspire greatly, who did make a difference, and whose lives make a good read.[8]

---

[6] John P. Davis., ed., *The American Negro Reference Book* (Englewood Cliffs, NJ: Prentice-Hall, Inc., 1966), 72; John Hope Franklin, *From Slavery to Freedom*, 5th edition (New York: Alfred A. Knopf, Inc., 1980 (1947)), 417; John Egerton, *Speak Now Against The Day: The Generation Before the Civil Rights Movement* (New York: Alfred A. Knopf, 1994), 458; Catherine Fosl, *Subversive Southerner: Anne Braden and the Struggle for Racial Justice in the Cold War South* (New York: Palgrave Macmillan, 2004), 140.

[7] Nell Irvin Painter, *The Narrative of Hosea Hudson: His Life as Negro Communist in the South* (Cambridge, MA, London, UKP: Harvard University Press, 1979), 28.

[8] Tugwell quoted in Thomas Kessner, *Fiorello H. LaGuardia and the Making of Modern New York* (New York: McGraw Hill Publishing Company, 1989), xvi.

Foreword

MICHAEL H. NASH

The idea for this collection of essays originated at an October 28, 2006 symposium, "James and Esther Jackson, the American Left and the Origins of the Modern Civil Rights Movement." Organized by New York University to announce the Tamiment Library's acquisition of the James and Esther Jackson papers, this all-day event brought together nearly 200 professional historians, students, civil rights activists, current and former members of the Communist Party to hear and comment on a wide range of papers dealing with the early years of the civil rights movement, the careers of James and Esther Jackson, the Southern Negro Youth Congress, and the role of the Communist Party. Pete Seeger, who had helped organize the Caravan Puppeteers to support James Jackson and the Southern Negro Youth Congress's voter registration work in Alabama in 1939 and 1940, came with his banjo to share some of the songs from that campaign with the audience. Former Manhattan Borough President Percy Sutton arrived unannounced and spoke about his brother's relationship with James Jackson, the African-American leadership of the Communist Party, and the civil rights movement during World War II.

Today, the Southern Negro Youth Congress (SNYC) is largely forgotten; however, in the 1930s and 1940s it was in the forefront of the struggle for racial equality as it was one of the first organizations since the end of Reconstruction to challenge the Southern Jim Crow system of racial segregation. Organized in 1937 in Richmond, Virginia by James E. Jackson and several hundred activists, the SNYC built an inter-racial movement that brought students and working people together in a struggle for civil rights and economic justice. The SNYC addressed issues of race, class, gender, and democratic citizenship that are still with us today. Nearly three decades before the Student Non-Violent Coordinating Committee, the SNYC in a proclamation written by James Jackson declared: "We have a right to a school that is free and equal; to a home around which the spectre of poverty, sickness and want does not hover, to playgrounds and swimming pools .... We have a right to jobs at equal pay for equal work ...."

While the SNYC disappeared after World War II, one of the many casualties of the McCarthy period, James and Esther Jackson remained important figures in the struggle for African American equality for more than

FIG. 1. James E. Jackson, Jr. at the Southern Negro Youth Congress Banquet, Birmingham, Alabama, 1942.

FIG. 2. James E. Jackson, Jr., the last American journalist to interview Ho Chi Minh before his death, 1968.

FIG. 3. **Esther Cooper leads a Civil Rights Congress demonstration to free Carl
Winter at the federal building in Michigan, September 16, 1949.**

sixty years. After serving in the army during World War II, James Jackson
worked as a civil rights, labor, and Communist Party organizer in New Orleans
and Detroit. In 1951 he was one of 21 Communist Party leaders indicted under
the Smith Act. His conspiracy conviction was unanimously reversed by a
federal appeals court in a 1958 decision that was based on the Supreme Court
ruling in *Yates v. United States*; the mere teaching or advocacy of an overthrow
of the government did not constitute a "call to action." Jackson later became
educational director for the Communist Party and editor of the *Daily Worker*.
He was the last American reporter to interview Ho Chi Minh shortly before
his death in 1968.

Esther Cooper Jackson served as executive-secretary of the Southern Negro
Youth Congress during World War II. Later she worked for the Michigan
branch of the Civil Rights Congress. She was an organizer for the Committee to
Defend Negro Leadership, whose purpose was to support African-Americans
under attack during the McCarthy period. In 1961 she was part of the group
that founded with Dr. W.E.B. Du Bois *Freedomways* magazine where she was
managing editor for 25 years.

The Jackson papers and the essays in this volume speak to the renewed interest in civil rights history that point to a long movement beginning in the 1930s. They tell us much about the struggle for racial equality during the depression decade and World War II era and the ways that struggle was linked to issues of class and gender. In a 1985 oral history interview (with Robin Kelley), Esther Cooper Jackson said that being an African-American Communist in the South meant "struggling with the issue of gender." As Sara Rzeszutek's essay shows the civil rights struggle saw women and men working together in ways that stretched the boundaries of traditional gender roles. The movement was built on a coalition of labor unionists, civil rights activists, idealistic students, Communists, and New Dealers who began the struggle to reform the South and re-enfranchise black people. This is the story told in this book and in the Jackson papers.

Nine of the ten chapters are based on papers, substantially revised, delivered at the October 2006 symposium. Timothy Johnson's essay was commissioned by the editors for this volume. The first two essays by Robin Kelley and David Levering Lewis assess and contextualize the Jacksons' lives and careers. They also highlight the ways in which the Jackson archive will "open new vistas for studying the American left [and] the Black freedom movement" that call the traditional civil rights narrative into question. The next series of essays by Robert Korstad, Johnetta Richards, and Erik McDuffie discuss civil rights unionism, the Southern Negro Youth Congress, radical black feminism, and the role of the Communist Party. The essay by Michael Anderson on Lorraine Hansberry provides a link between the civil rights struggles of the 1930s and 1940s and the movement of the 1960s. Lorraine Hansberry, who came of age working with Paul Robeson and Louis Burnham at *Freedom* magazine and went on to write *Raisin in the Sun*, makes this connection perfectly. The essay on the development of the journal *Freedomways* brings the story into the 1970s. Angela Davis' closing essay connects these threads and relates the past to the present.

This collection of essays does not claim to be a comprehensive treatment of the civil rights movement of the 1930s and 1940s. There is little discussion of the Southern Conference for Human Welfare that many scholars think was at least as important as the Southern Negro Youth Congress. The book is also mostly silent about the role of the New Deal, the Congress of Industrial Organizations, and the Henry Wallace campaign. Nevertheless, I believe this volume will be an important contribution to the history of the civil rights movement, as it resurrects the Southern Negro Youth Congress in ways that connect the pre-war and post-war civil rights history.

The Tamiment Library was pleased to host the 2006 symposium and play a role in the publication of this volume. Tamiment is one of the most important special collections in the United States that preserves the history of the American left and labor movement. Shortly after the James and Esther Jackson papers arrived, Tamiment acquired the records of the Communist Party, USA and the Library of its Reference Center for Marxist Studies. These collections will support generations of scholarship about the American radical tradition, the history of communism, labor, and civil rights activism.

This volume has been nearly four years in the making and many debts have been incurred along the way. Besides Esther Jackson (James is no longer with us), thanks are due to Professor David Levering Lewis and to Timothy Johnson, Africana Studies Librarian at NYU, who were part of the team that organized the conference and then helped put this book together. Professor Lewis introduced me to James and Esther Jackson. Without his help and support this project never would have taken place. Dan Leab of *American Communist History* made this publication happen. He took the manuscript on faith and helped shape a collection of essays into a book.

Introduction

DAVID LEVERING LEWIS

"Why isn't it common knowledge," asks historian Robin Kelley, that James and Esther Jackson were precursors to "virtually all national civil rights organizations?" "Why aren't they household names?" Kelley adds. The eleven contributors to this commemorative edition respond to the first question by providing, as does Professor Kelley himself, a comprehensive public and personal knowledge base to insure that the extraordinary accomplishments of this singular husband and wife duo escape the neglect and obscurity that American history reserves for so many of its progressive pathfinders. The men and women who sustained the ideals and crafted the politics of the American left struggled heroically against the grain of the exceptionalist ideology that was dominant through much of the modern era—and greatly intensified in the military-industrial-complex reality after World War II. The national election of 1946, like that of 1896, delivered a crippling blow to the prospects of the economic democracy for which James and Esther Jackson fought with such selfless discipline and admirable integrity.

Tim Johnson reminds us that the Jacksons did indeed "make history," along with their colleagues, Edward Strong, Louis Burnham, "and others too many to mention." They organized black tobacco workers in Richmond, Virginia, demonstrated against lynching and agitated for minority voting rights, and, as Professor Erik McDuffie reveals, Esther Jackson's out-of-the-box empirical study of "Negro Women Domestic Workers in Relation to Trade Unionism" was integral to "an emergent black feminism." The couple added to the history of the left by organizing with several others at Howard University in 1936 the foundational Southern Negro Youth Congress (SNYC) whose Columbia, South Carolina, convention ten years later inspired W.E.B. Du Bois's memorable keynote address, "Behold the Land."

Again, though, this was progressive history-making that dropped out of the civil rights narrative until its recent recovery by a new generation of less partisan historians. Although the SNYC was "one of many casualties of the post-war red scare," Professor Richards documents a legacy "that contributed to the civil rights movement of the 1960s." To which legacy must be added, as Professor Angela Davis's cogent symposium keynote emphasizes, Jim and Esther Jackson's informed resistance to "what we might call the seductions of black nationalism" that all too often came at the expense of economic empowerment.

FIG. 4. *The Southern Negro Youth Conference Summons You* to the Southern Youth Legislature, from the 7th Southern Negro Youth Conference Souvenir Journal, Columbia, South Carolina, October 18–21, 1946.

But let us underscore why the dogged, durable, and heroic achievements of the Jacksons have been historically problematic—"why," as Robin Kelley asks, "aren't the Jacksons household names?" As Tim Johnson underscores, "the context of their actions was their membership or association with the Communist Party of the United States." He might well have expanded upon that fact by observing that the honorands of this symposium suffered the charge of "un-American activities" by which generations of good and true citizens have been stigmatized and their aspirations demonized. "We devoted ourselves to each other, to our daughters, and to the great causes of our times," Maurice Jackson remembers his mentors telling him time and again. "All those dreams we cherish" is the leitmotif of those poignant letters the couple exchanged, a rich correspondence trove exemplifying gender co-equality in marriage, as Sara Rzeszutek's contribution wonderfully discloses. *Freedomways* bears Esther's imprint of progressive dynamism, the magazine that, for a quarter century, was, as Ms. Jean Bond recalled at the NYU symposium "inextricable from what people were creating and struggling to achieve on the ground." Michael Anderson's profile of contributor Lorraine Hansberry recaptures something of the startup excitement of *Freedomways*.

The gratifying and timely success of these eleven essays presents James and Esther Jackson in the public and personal fullness of their authentic American odyssey. We may be reasonably encouraged that the time has come when, as Robin Kelley hopes, students will never again assume that mention of "the Jacksons" has anything to do with Michael and Janet.

The Jacksons

ROBIN D. G. KELLEY

It is time to mark a long overdue acknowledgement of the crucial role the Jacksons played in struggles for social justice, and the gift of their papers to the Tamiment library should open new vistas for studying the American Left, and the Black freedom movement, not to mention literary and cultural developments. While we must acknowledge all the work that has yet to be done, it is important to recognize the tremendous scholarship produced since my *Hammer and Hoe* was published sixteen years ago: we've witnessed some amazing work on Southern radicalism—Patricia Sullivan, Robert Korstad, Michael Honey, Dianne McWhorter, and Gerald Zahavi, not to mention work on the Jacksons and the Communist Party more broadly by Gerald Home, Erik McDuffie, Dayo Gore, Sarah Hart Brown, and Carol Anderson. And before I got into the mix, Johnetta Richards had written an important dissertation on the Southern Negro Youth Congress.

I met James Jackson, Jr. on September 26, 1986, in the Communist Party office on W. 23rd St. —and at the time I was living in California. I remember that first interview quite fondly. He was very busy at the time and when we made the initial arrangements I think he only had 45 minutes to spare. We ended up talking almost three hours. I've never asked him this, but I think he was a little surprised (perhaps pleasantly?) that I was black. In those days, besides Gerald Home who really pioneered this scholarship, there weren't a whole lot of young black scholars interested in the Communist Party.

In any case, the first forty minutes of the interview was essentially a speech— he laid out the objective conditions in the South at the time and presented the Party's strategy and tactics, and gave a wonderful capsule history of the Southern Negro Youth Congress. But then I pushed him to talk about himself and his personal experiences in Virginia, in Birmingham, in the rural areas. And then he really opened up—talked fondly about his friendship with Louis

Burnham, talked about how he taught sharecroppers dialectics through the natural growth of cotton; he revealed the difficulty and danger of organizing a movement in Birmingham in the late 1930s, and though I never used them, he told fascinating stories about his military intelligence work in Burma.

I should note that when I interviewed James Jackson the first time, I had yet to travel to Alabama. I headed South in November of that year, and the archives I encountered and interviews I conducted changed my thinking about the project dramatically, and what I found helped me to better understand what James Jackson was trying to tell me: that the Communist Party's presence in Alabama was as much about intellectual work and developing critical analysis among workers and sharecroppers, as it was about challenging police repression, Jim Crow, forced evictions, and below-poverty wages.

By the time I met Esther Cooper Jackson, I had spent considerable time in the South and read virtually every scrap of paper dealing with the Southern Negro Youth Congress. When I visited her in their Brooklyn apartment, I was prepared with more pointed questions and detailed information. What I remember, however, is that she began by interviewing me! She wanted to know who I was, who my people were, why on earth was I interested in Communists? At first, I didn't know if she was just being the great journalist/editor that she is, or just being suspicious in light of having endured decades of police and FBI surveillance and repression, or was just curious. Once we got rolling, however, she offered me incredibly rich insights into the culture of the movement, the black and interracial community they created, relations between men and women in the movement, and her own personal journey to becoming a revolutionary. I recall being particularly struck with her description of the coterie of young black radical couples in Birmingham who worked consciously to eradicate sexism within their households. Esther talked about how she and her husband, Ed Strong and Augusta Jackson Strong, and Louis and Dorothy Burnham attempted to share housework and childrearing duties, as well as public speaking and organizational leadership. Unlike so many other social justice organizations, the women were not chained to mimeograph machines. As Esther explained to me then, the men "actually thought [that] to be a good Communist you struggled on the woman question."

In other words, the historical lessons I learned from the Jacksons and the movements of which they were a part overturned virtually all of my assumptions about black radicals in the South. I was raised on the traditional Civil Rights narrative—the story of a silent South suddenly coming to life after Brown v. Board of Education or the Montgomery Bus Boycott. I discovered quickly just how much history had been repressed by McCarthyite repression and good old-fashioned racism. Even when I set out to write *Hammer and Hoe: Alabama Communists During the Great Depression*, I didn't realize the degree to which groups like the Southern Negro Youth Congress took on white supremacy head-on. (In fact, I'm still amazed that there is no book on the SNYC!).

Indeed, what I found most striking about the Jacksons was that they, along with the Strongs, the Burnhams, Thelma Dale, Sallye Davis, and several others, represented a community of young, black, visionary intellectuals who chose to settle in Birmingham in order to challenge white supremacy and racial capitalism at its core. They were middle-class intellectuals, largely but not entirely Southern-born, who could have charted a different future for themselves, but instead chose to "commit class suicide," if you will, and devote their lives to the struggles of working people and the disfranchised. James Jackson was a young pharmacy student pursuing an M.S. degree at Howard University. A native of Richmond, Virginia, born in 1914 "into a cultured family in comfortable circumstances," Jackson had become a rebel at a very young age. He fought racism and segregation in the Boy Scouts, joined the Communist Party at sixteen, and as a student organized Virginia Union University's first Marxist club. With the help of black Detroit Communist Christopher Columbus Alston, he spent the summer of 1936 planning the first Southern Negro Youth Congress, which was subsequently held in Richmond, Virginia, February 13–14, 1937, to coincide with Frederick Douglass' birthday.

No sooner had the conference concluded when Alston and Jackson were approached by local tobacco workers to help organize a union. The workers, mostly female, were desperate since the AFL Tobacco Workers' International Union refused to support their strike. Before the year was up, the pair had organized the Tobacco Stemmers' and Laborers' Industrial Union, which launched a successful sit-down strike in Richmond's British American Tobacco Company resulting in significant wage increases, union recognition, and a 40 hour week. Within months the union established seven locals and claimed a membership of several thousand Richmond tobacco workers.

In 1939, after holding their third annual conference in Birmingham (the second was in Chattanooga), the SNYC leadership decided to move their head office there. Jackson and Ed Strong felt that Birmingham was ripe for a radical movement of young people allied with the city's organized black working class. They both relocated there, and a year later were joined by Esther Cooper, who was brought on to serve as office director and administrative secretary. Born in Arlington, Virginia, in 1917, Cooper was the daughter of a school teacher (also a leading voice in the local NAACP) and a U.S. Army officer. Educated in Washington, D.C., public schools, she enrolled in Oberlin College in 1934. By her sophomore year, Cooper had been drawn to several political organizations, including the Fellowship of Reconciliation and the American Students Union, and she attended a few YCL meetings.

Graduating in 1938, Cooper continued her studies at Fisk—at the behest of distinguished social scientist Charles S. Johnson—to pursue an M.A. Degree in Sociology. There she met a small coterie of Communist professors, mostly white, who brought her into their inner circle. Meanwhile, she remained active in student politics, joining the Student Christian Association and attending SNYC's historic Birmingham conference in 1939. By the time Cooper graduated in 1940, she was highly sought after for her scholarly as well as political endeavors. Her master's thesis on domestic workers and unions earned her a scholarship to pursue a Ph.D. at the University of Chicago (under the direction of Sociologist Robert Park). At the same time, Ed Strong and James Jackson asked her to run the new Birmingham office. Choosing to do so, Cooper moved to Birmingham in July 1940 and gave up a promising academic career. Of course, her decision to accept the SNYC's offer was primarily political, but there were personal considerations as well... I'll just leave it at that.

Clearly, there is much more to the Jacksons' early stories, but my main point is to illustrate the choices they made in terms of their lives and careers. Esther might have been a leading sociologist of race and class; James might have been a very successful pharmacist and proprietor of his own drugstore. But they chose a different path, made no money but made history.

When we think about the community they created within SNYC, the Jacksons were surrounded by folks who made similar choices. Besides the Burnhams and the Strongs, we might consider Sallye Davis, a young school teacher originally from Talldega who graduated Miles Memorial College the year SNYC established its headquarters in Birmingham, and Thelma Dale, a sociology student at Howard who happened to be the niece of Tuskegee Institute president F.D. Patterson.

Although SNYC and the League of Young Southerners (the white counterpart to SNYC), grew organically out of the conditions of Birmingham at the time, there is a way in which even the most sympathetic readers of *Hammer and Hoe* dismiss the Popular Front period as fundamentally less militant and less interesting. Most readers emphasize the Third period, the underground—they like the idea of these semi-literate steel workers and sharecroppers building a movement rooted in a kind of folk culture. But as I said in the book, SNYC represented an even more confrontational politics, and more directly laid the foundations for the modern Civil Rights movement.

While it is true that I suggest that the Party in Alabama tried to build alliances with unwilling Southern white liberals at the expense of working-class organizing, this was NOT the case with the SNYC, whose leaders maintained those links, promoted their own version of a Double-V Campaign, and fought on many fronts alongside the black working class.

For example, they challenged Jim Crow on the buses: Mildred McAdory led a group of five SNYC activists to protest segregation on public transportation in Fairfield (a suburb of Birmingham), for which she was beaten and arrested. As a result of the incident, the SNYC formed a short-lived organization called the Citizens Committee for Equal Accommodations on Common Carriers.

They also battled and exposed incidents of police brutality.

And fought tirelessly for voting rights: launching a mass voter registration campaign and an anti-poll tax drive, in alliance with both the CIO and the NAACP. The Congress's basic demands included the elimination of the poll tax, white primaries, and various literacy requirements, as well as complete protection from physical violence and other forms of intimidation blacks had to endure at polling booths. Under the auspices of the Right to Vote Club that black Communists had formed initially, Ed Strong, Esther Cooper and James Jackson instituted workshops to educate potential voters of their rights with respect to the poll-tax, property qualifications, and voter registration for veterans. Congress organizers also tried to reach workers in the mines owned by the Tennessee Coal and Iron Company, but company police posed a formidable barrier. At the Hamilton Slope mine, for example, police arrested James and Esther for distributing anti-poll tax literature to miners.

Finally, this community of black radical intellectuals launched a cultural and artistic revolution anticipating both the modern Civil Rights movement and the Black Arts Movement. They published a literary arts magazine called *Cavalcade*, organized literacy programs for urban and rural working people, sponsored art and musical events, and developed a people's theater as well as a traveling puppet show called the "Caravan Puppeteers," which staged performances about voting rights, citizenship, strike-breaking, democracy, and black history.

So clearly, the Jacksons and their comrades in Birmingham were the precursors to movements like the Alabama Christian Movement for Human Rights under the leadership of Fred Shuttlesworth, not to mention virtually all national civil rights organizations. Why isn't this common knowledge and why aren't they household names?

The immediate and most obvious answer has to do with anti-Communism. Even before the McCarthy era, the SNYC was red-baited from within its ranks. The issue came up at its 4th annual conference in New Orleans in 1940, when some adult advisors unsuccessfully tried to persuade the organization to pass resolutions restricting participation of Communists.

The organization lasted until 1948, but by then the Jacksons had left Birmingham. James Jackson became chairman of the CPUSA in Louisiana, but because of red-baiting and death threats, they were forced to flee to Detroit. There he organized auto workers at Ford's Dearborn plant and Esther led the Michigan branch of the Civil Rights Congress. They were eventually forced completely underground when James was wanted by the FBI under the Smith Act.

FIG. 1. James E. Jackson, Jr. (third from the left) leading a demonstration against police brutality in Detroit, June 11, 1948.

The Cold War can only go so far as an explanation for their historical absence: it is up to us to make their stories known and to create a world where I can mention "the Jacksons" to my students and they don't assume I'm talking about Michael or Janet.

James and Esther Jackson: A Historical Assessment

DAVID LEVERING LEWIS

Somewhere in the vast literature of the American Left is the observation that a quite significant percentage of African-Americans who belonged to the Communist Party of the United States were upper middle class. This was a counterintuitive proposition someone or somehow shared with me long before I began research for a life-and-times biography of W.E.B. Du Bois. I guard a vivid memory of the setting in which the upper middle-class character of many men and women of color committed to the cause of scientific socialism really struck home. John Pittman was a Morehouse College graduate, with a Master's in economics from Berkeley, and a year at Stanford University Law School before landing a position as editor of San Francisco's black weekly, *The Spokesman*. Labor conditions in Great Depression San Francisco radicalized the young newspaperman who soon placed the newspaper at the service of the local Communist Party. Ideologically, Pittman never looked back. He served as *Daily Worker* correspondent in Europe after World War II, then as founding co-editor in 1968 of the *Daily World* and contributing editor to the journal *Political Affairs*.

Like myself, the 83-year-old John Pittman once called Atlanta, Georgia, home. When I interviewed him some time in 1989, this longtime associate of Esther and James Jackson had only recently returned to the United States from Prague after a decade of service as correspondent for the *Worker*. As we discussed this courtly, sophisticated man's career in an office at the national Communist Party headquarters in lower Manhattan, it dawned on me that John Pittman personified a curious Talented Tenth political phenomenon, exemplars of which soon came crowding into my awareness—men and women such as Amherst College and Harvard Law graduate, and CPUSA official, Benjamin J. Davis, Jr., or social scientist Doxey Wilkerson, or English literature professor Alphaeus Hunton, or Newspaper Guild activist Marvel Cooke, or Yale-trained dramatist and writer, Shirley Graham. They were Du Bois's god-children, and as his intellectual progeny it should not surprise us that they found their way early on to the same progressive politics their godfather would ultimately embrace in the last two decades of his life.

To the extent that this counter-intuitive insight is valid, its large and enduring meaning emerges spectacularly even from an abbreviated historical assessment of Esther Cooper and James Edward Jackson, Jr. Consider the implications of this salient fact: Jim and Esther Jackson were mid-20th century facilitators of the ideological evolution of one of America's sharpest and boldest public intellectuals. To be sure, as the novelist Howard Fast once cautioned, no one ever successfully pushed W.E.B. Du Bois to take a position against his will. But the Jacksons were there with political convictions shaped by rich experience and a reassuring sociability in bad times to accompany Du Bois on his questing way leftward. You may remember that Du Bois said once that had he died at age fifty, his death would have occasioned much lamentation and many eulogies, but that at age seventy his death was "practically requested." In striking contrast to the profile of most lives, Du Bois was to become increasingly anti-establishmentarian, so that at age 95 he was more radically unorthodox than virtually any other engaged intellectual, black or white, of the 20th century. At seventy in 1938, however, Du Bois's significant ideological interaction with the Jacksons was yet some seven or eight years in the future; and where Du Bois was heading Esther and Jim had long been in residence ever since, to borrow from Robert Cohen's apt title, *The Old Left Was Young.*

But who were these Jacksons before they became the dream team of the revolutionary left? The answer to that question is profoundly intriguing and instructive. It was of course all about the color line that was famously proclaimed as the problem of the last century. As we shall see, the biographies of both Jacksons amply validate the Du Boisian prophecy. Yet what their biographies also admirably exemplify is a precocious linking of color to class and gender and of all three to America's historically programmatic mal-distribution of wealth and resources. Some may say that the coming of age under Jim Crow of James Edward Jackson and Esther Victoria Cooper inevitably propelled them beyond the civil rights Fabianism of their peers into a life of militant international socialism. That is for you to judge.

Esther Cooper's father, George Posia Cooper, a Virginian, fought with Theodore Roosevelt's Rough Riders in Cuba, served with the US Army of occupation in the Philippines, commanded troops in France as a lieutenant in the Great War, and retired at the same rank in 1928 to accept employment in the Bureau of Printing and Engraving in Washington. Ex-cavalry officer Cooper continued to ride horseback at Fort Myer, and to fill the family home in Arlington with books—encyclopedias, the Harvard Classics, and of course every copy of *The Crisis*. Father's pride in his three daughters' solid education was exuberant. "He was the kind of father who would clap louder—embarrass us, even in grade school," Professor Sarah Hart Brown quotes Esther as saying in the fine essay found in *Lives Full of Struggle and Triumph* from the University Press of Florida.

Mother was an outstanding role model. Esther Irving Cooper was a stenographer, teacher, and community activist. She was a fine musician, brilliant at civil service exams (the US Forest Service accepted her reluctantly when it discovered her race), and a change agent in Washington's notoriously prim and proper colored society. Mother taught business subjects at Nannie Helen Burroughs' National School for Women and Girls. Along her busy way, Mother helped found the ecumenical group Church Women United, headed the Arlington black PTA, and served as an officer in the American Legion Auxiliary. She energized the local branch of the NAACP, and narrowly lost out in a race to become a national Democratic Committeewoman. In 1939, Mother organized picketing of the premier of *Gone With the Wind*.

Esther Jackson and her sisters attended Washington's prestigious Dunbar High School–a virtual conveyor belt ran from segregated Dunbar to the Ivy Leagues and the elite colleges. A first rate monograph is still badly needed for that forcing house of the Talented Tenth. Oberlin came next, her great aunt's college, and still committed to a correct and cool reception of students of color. Our student gravitated—no surprise there—to the campus socialists and progressives, to the pacifist Fellowship of Reconciliation, and to a major in sociology. Lieutenant Cooper died proudly anticipating attending his daughter's 1938 graduation with honors only weeks away. The following year finds Esther on a full scholarship to study sociology at Fisk University under the formidable Charles S. Johnson.

Academically, Fisk more than met its promise with an outstanding interracial faculty among which numbered Aaron Douglas of Harlem Renaissance renown and the Robisons, a white faculty couple of decided leftist persuasions. Indeed, the Fisk Esther Jackson got to know, rather sounds like City College in its red salad days. There was this band of professors at Fisk and Tennessee A&I State College who ran a Marxist study group. "That's how I first started reading some of this literature," she recalls. "They would see students in their classes who had expressed opinions or ideas and they'd invite them over. One professor ... had what I called a little 'Anne Frank' room—he kept all kinds of literature and would invite those students he was impressed with to read the literature." Our sociologist chose to live in a Methodist Settlement House off campus where she worked with black families in the neighborhood. The experience was both intellectually and existentially lasting in much the same way as Fisk undergraduate Du Bois's famous two summers teaching in the Tennessee backcountry. "Seeing these conditions," she concluded that "no small amount of change would do." The Nashville experience together with a research stint in New York interviewing working class white women, "steer[ed] me to radical politics," says Esther, by the time she received her Fisk master's degree in 1940.

Esther Cooper, Oberlin alumna with a master's degree in sociology from Fisk under Charles Johnson, was twenty seven. Her career path to a doctorate at the University of Chicago veered suddenly one afternoon when asked to show a handsome, visiting Carnegie-Myrdal researcher around the Fisk campus. James Jackson had been engaged by Ralph Bunche to conduct field research for

Gunnar Myrdal's massive race relations project, to be published in 1944 as *An American Dilemma*. We learn that the serious Fisk visitor fell asleep on their first movie date, but the electricity of commitment passing between them was high voltage. When the fateful invitation arrived to come to Birmingham, Alabama, to join the Southern Negro Youth Congress (SNYC) voter registration drive organized by its Executive Secretary James Jackson and Edward Strong, Esther gladly heeded her mother's counsel ("go ahead, try it") and relinquished a coveted Rosenwald Fellowships study with Robert Park at Chicago. In marrying James Edward Jackson in 1941, Esther Cooper married one of the most committed intellectual activists of his generation, and she also married the Communist Party. When the National Committee of the CPUSA honored him in 2003, its executive secretary's much overdue commendation stated that "Jim Jackson's lifetime is a record of enormous practical and theoretical contributions to the working-class movement."

Let us now meet James Edward Jackson, Jr., of Richmond, Virginia's Jackson Ward—Jackson, for "Stonewall", that is, for people of color in the capital of the former Confederacy were daily reminded that the South was rising on their backs. Jackson and his four siblings nevertheless benefited from the special environment and advantages that his father and six other determined professional men created within a *Plessy v. Ferguson* universe. Richmond's residential segregation was almost absolute. Blacks were not even permitted to walk the streets of affluent neighborhoods. Jackson *père* and his colleagues pooled capital to buy 2 dilapidated white-owned farms on the edge of the city. Forming the Frederick Douglass Realty Company in 1925, the men parceled the farm into lots for upscale homes. Jim Jackson grew up in a large brick house in Frederick Douglass Court where the streets were named Du Bois, Dunbar, Tubman, Langston, and such like.

Jackson *père*, a pharmacist, reared his children on a steady diet of readings from "As the Crow Flies", the young people's section of *The Crisis*. Like many Talented Tenth children, Jim Jackson bore a ten-year-old's memory of a Du Bois's visit to tree-lined Du Bois Avenue. Mrs. Jackson emerged from frenzied preparation of her finest cooking, to be told by the distinguished, perverse, guest, "Madam, I will have a slice of cheese on toast and a glass of milk, thank you."

Read Joel Willliamson's *Crucible of Race*, Leon Litwack's *Trouble in Mind*, or Charles Payne's *I've Got the Light of Freedom*, to be reminded of the plethora of small and large humiliations essential to the policing of black aspirations. The gross insult visited upon the teenage Jim Jackson might have scarred his psyche a lifetime. Since Boy Scout chapters were closed to black Virginians, Jim, Spottswood Robinson III (who would be part of the Marshall team arguing *Brown v. Board of Education*), and several other adolescents petitioned the national organization for a segregated chapter, Troop 75 B. By the time Jim enrolled at Virginia Union University at sixteen, he had accomplished the notable feat of becoming the first and only Negro Eagle Scout in the entire South. His medal was to be presented at a widely reported Richmond public occasion by the governor.

FIG. 1. James E. Jackson, Jr., age 16, first black Eagle Scout in the South, October 1931.

Medals were pinned on the dozen or so white Scouts. But the governor of Virginia tossed the medal to the young man in the presence of Jackson's parents. Pinning his own medal to his chest and saluting as the abashed whites limply began to applaud, Eagle Scout Jackson took his first steps leftward. He joined the Young Communist League (YCL) not long afterward. Three quick years at Virginia Union were followed, after 1934, by another accelerated course of study at Howard University's School of Pharmacy.

Like Esther's years at Fisk, Jim's at Howard were characterized by stellar academics and purposeful engagement with campus radicals. This was that golden age of Howard's serious faculty socialism described in Jonathan Holloway's *Confronting the Veil: Abram Harris, Jr., E. Franklin Frazier, and Ralph Bunche, 1919–1941.* Although Jackson was a member of the YCL and a founding member of the Southern Negro Youth Congress (SNYC) organized at Howard in his second year, he appears to have restrained his activism somewhat for the sake of professional school studies. No record exists of participation in the off-campus Marxist bull sessions at Harrison's Grill, where some of the left's future stalwarts cut their ideological eye-teeth. Back in Richmond in partnership with his father in 1937, though, the new pharmacist and his SNYC cadre made organizing history as the Richmond vanguard of the CIO's push to unionize tobacco workers, the most appallingly treated of whom were black women. The Richmond efforts succeeded after several hard fought strikes, with more than 5,000 workers winning union recognition. Robin Kelley has told much of this story in his classic, *Hammer and Hoe.*

Jackson worked as a Party organizer until his induction into the army in 1943. By then, he had contributed significantly to the Carnegie-Myrdal study, met and married Esther Cooper and together produced a daughter, Harriet (their other daughter, Kathryn Alice, was to be born some years later). Jackson carried the fight against segregation to Birmingham as SNYC's National Director of Education, collaborated with southern white youth groups, and sponsored a SNYC conference addressed by Howard's combative president, Mordecai Johnson, and several other prominent members of the African-American political class whose mounting impatience with the racial status quo was documented in Rayford Logan's seminal 1944 edition, *What the Negro Wants.* When Sergeant Jackson returned home from duty in the 823 Aviation Engineer battalion in Burma to be discharged in early 1946, he learned that his wife of five years had sailed for the World Youth Conference in London, after which she would travel to Russia to work as a bricklayer's assistant in the rebuilding of Stalingrad. Harriet was left with grandparents.

Esther Jackson and W.E.B. Du Bois finally met for the first time in London. In a sense, the father of Pan Africanism had run to London to catch up with the Zeitgeist set in motion by his own ideas and programs forty years earlier. George Padmore and his generation had presumed to organize a fifth Pan African Congress in Manchester, England, with scarcely more than perfunctory consultation with the great man. For Du Bois, as for Paul Robeson, the overthrow of European colonialism was integral to the advancement of domestic civil rights and vice versa. He considered the National Negro Congress, the Council for African Affairs, the National Lawyers Guild, and other militant organizations sponsored by the leftwing labor unions within the CIO as welcome allies in the struggle.

At Manchester, Padmore handed the opening session's gavel to Du Bois as the Congress's honorary president. Young Kwame Nkrumah served as rapporteur. Jomo Kenyatta spoke for East Africa; Peter Abrahams for South Africa; Ras Makonnen for Ethiopia. Previous Congress manifestos had called on Europeans to honor their own ideals of liberty and justice. The Manchester manifesto warned them of the coming payback. "Yet if the western world is still determined to rule mankind by force," said Du Bois and the collective authors, "then Africans, as a last resort, may have to appeal to force in order to achieve freedom, even if force destroys them and the world." On this portentous note, Du Bois departed Manchester in late October 1945 to renew old pre-war acquaintances. But it was not encounters with aged Fabians but his meeting with young black American Communists from middle-class backgrounds that was the highlight of his London stay. Thousands of young people had converged on London from Europe, India, China, and the western hemisphere for the founding meeting of the World Youth Conference, a rejuvenating experience that brought into Du Bois's life a vivacious young woman of stunning intelligence and poise.

The Southern Negro Youth Congress (SNYC) delegates in London were led by executive secretary Esther Jackson. Impressed, Du Bois accepted her invitation to meet a small group of representative SNYC-ers at a dinner she cooked for the lot. Although he vaguely recalled an invitation to be keynote speaker at a SNYC convention several years ago, until meeting Jackson Du Bois had known little more about the organization than that it had begun at Howard in 1936 under the auspices of the National Negro Congress. They were committed to unity across racial lines and to bringing fundamental economic change to the South, Jackson explained. Du Bois was much impressed by an internationalist language seldom if ever heard before, he thought, from African American young people. Du Bois submitted a report to the NAACP of his English mission that spoke of the SNYC as a major social force in the making and of Esther Jackson's organizational aptitude and remarkable political intelligence. Gloster Current, the hardworking executive director of the NAACP, Detroit branch, had attended the World Youth Conference as NAACP head Walter White's special emissary. The more conservative Current had been selected abruptly to replace Ruby Hurley, the national youth secretary, after new board member Eleanor Roosevelt raised concerns about the large Soviet presence expected to attend the conclave. Current was crushed to find no mention of himself in Du Bois's report, but to White and his associate Roy Wilkins the omission was organizationally and politically heinous. Asked to amend his report, Du Bois let his secretary refuse for him. Roy Wilkins fumed to White: "You know that we suspected at the beginning that this Youth Conference, and particularly the American delegation might be a communist front group," Who had ever heard of this Esther Cooper Jackson who had been preferred over the expert Gloster Current?

Upon his 1946 discharge from the army, Jim Jackson wrote to Du Bois asking for an interview, perhaps at the suggestion of Esther in a letter from Europe. Jackson had followed Du Bois's evolving thought. He remembers four or five sessions, each lasting exactly an hour and forty-five minutes in Du Bois's Harlem apartment. Thirty-two-year-old James Jackson, on orders from the Party's national secretariat, assumed the challenge of encouraging W.E.B. Du Bois to enter the Communist fold despite the good doctor's amused insistence that he was simply a "bourgeois democrat." Engaged by the theoretical bent of Jackson's mind, confirmed in his World Youth Conference estimate of Esther Jackson, and equally impressed now by City College radical Louis Burnham and SNYC co-founder Ed Strong, Du Bois accepted an invitation to address the SNYC conference that October in the South Carolina capital.

His decision to accept the invitation to deliver the keynote address to the seventh southeast SNYC conference meeting in Columbia, South Carolina represented a major step toward revolutionary socialism, a step that Walter White, Roy Wilkins, and much of the NAACP board viewed with publicly unspoken disfavor. Whatever its ties to international communism, the SNYC was led by native-born Communists idealistically dedicated to bringing a better life to the black and white people of the wretchedly poor South. The organization's honorary president was none other than Frederick Patterson, president of Tuskegee Institute. To turn a page or two of Patterson's essay in *What the Negro Wants* was to sense the deep, contemporary civil rights impatience of a man whose distinguished position ten years earlier would have enforced Delphic circumspection. New Deal apparatchik Clark Foreman, president of the Southern Conference on Human Welfare (SCHW), was of the same mind as Patterson. Langston Hughes supported the organization from the beginning, writing *Don't You Want to Be Free?*, a one-act agit-prop play, mounted by SNYC units throughout the South. Adam Clayton Powell, Jr., spell-binding pastor of Harlem's Abyssinian Baptist Church and first of his race elected to Congress from the northeast, was also a supporter of the organization and expected to speak at the 1946 conference. (Powell failed inexplicably to participate.)

Introduced by a glowing Esther Jackson at the closing mass meeting on the evening of October 20, Du Bois spoke to 850 black and white delegates, joined by several hundred observers, in the crammed chapel of Benedict College. Paul Robeson and Howard Fast had spoken the night before. Du Bois's keynote address, printed as a fifteen-page pamphlet and reproduced in *New Masses*, was to become an instant classic of the left.

"Behold the Land" blended poetry and politics as it endeavored to refocus the struggle of the American Negro from the urban ghettos of the north and midwest to the cradle of the race. "The future of American Negroes is in the South," he said. The South was the "firing line" for the new struggle to emancipate not only American Negroes, Negroes of the West Indies, and Africans of the continent, but the "white slaves of modern capitalistic monopoly." He invited the audience to envisage the profound transformations possible under a new economic democracy based on interracial struggle that would emancipate both white and black youth of the region, "as brothers and sisters, as fellow travelers toward the dawn." Du Bois paid the young men and women of the Southern Negro Youth Congress a moving tribute. "Nothing" he had experienced in past years "has touched me more deeply," he wrote.

Back in New York, Walter White penned a long, offended memorandum when the text of "Behold the Land" reached him. Du Bois's "fellow travelers toward the dawn" were distinctly not to his liking, and he steamed over glowing references in the Chicago *Defender* to "young Negroes with guts" courageously meeting in the heart of the old Confederacy which ignored the NAACP's unprecedented and bold national convention held in Atlanta in 1920.

The coming paradigm was one of Cold War civil rights. Despite warnings from the NAACP establishment, Du Bois's sessions with James Jackson beginning in 1946 were the prelude to more frequent and politically rewarding associations with men and women on the left. Some of these new relationships came through Shirley Graham whose friendship with the immensely successful Communist writer Howard Fast had helped pave her way to recognition and modest financial income as a writer of biography and historical fiction. "Shirley made wonderful gumbo and she never stopped talking," Fast was fond of saying.

This was clearly a period of transition for Du Bois, the beginning of the final phase in the evolution of that divided self immemorially described by him at the beginning of the twentieth century. His ambitious Pan-African designs had privileged race—the solidarity of people of color—as the liberating *sine qua non* from the social and economic ills of this world: diasporic nationalism. Yet a shift of ideological emphasis was unmistakably evidenced by "Behold the Land" in its program of unity based on class rather than race. Simply stated, the central question for the twentieth century was whether economic empowerment and racial equality were possible under democratic liberalism, or whether economic egalitarianism was the logical prerequisite for liberal democracy and racial equality. Du Bois was himself in the process of deciding. *The World and Africa*, released by Viking Press in January 1947, reflected the divided thought of its author astride the fault line of nationalism and communism.

In the final analysis, Du Bois concluded that the United States was the problem of his century, whatever the failings of the Soviet Union. As for the great gains in civil rights for people of color—gains greatly due to his own magnificent inspiration and witness—he decided that they had been purchased at the price of collusion with the forces of global exploitation. Was there not paradox and irony in the scene of his last hours in New York before self-exile to Africa? Esther and Jim, having played their instrumental parts in the great man's political evolution, saw him off from Idlewild Airport and then returned to Brooklyn to continue the hard slog for incremental social democracy. Indeed, James Jackson's five-year disappearance into the Communist underground and 1956 Smith Act trial and conviction had been a major factor in the disgracefully belated invalidation of the Smith Act in *Yates v. United States*.

With Russia now ravaged by a phase of toxic capitalism that would repel Jay Gould and communism seemingly headed for history's curiosity shop of failed religions, some of Du Bois's pronouncements may appear to be painfully wrongheaded. But it is by far the significance of Du Bois's protest and of his gradual alienation, rather than the solutions he proposed, that are instructive. For he was an intellectual in the purest sense of the word—a thinker whose obligation was to be dissatisfied continually with his own thoughts and those of others. No doubt he was precipitous in totally writing off the market economy. Even so, it may be suggested that Du Bois was right to insist that to leave the solution of systemic social problems exclusively to the market is an agenda guaranteeing obscene economic inequality in the short run and political disaster in the long run.

In a real sense, as his evaluation of Martin Luther King's economic program revealed, W.E.B. Du Bois considered the civil rights struggle of the early sixties parochial, however important. Esther and Jim never did. For them, the local struggle and the global struggle were inseparable, and that was the message of the inaugural issue of *Freedomways*, a major venture in the advancement of progressivism. "This is a good world and a good time in which we were born," Esther and her co-editors announced: "Over a half million Negroes in the United States are participating in organizations formed to do away with discrimination, segregation, and to demand full citizenship rights," the editors trumpeted. What the magazine offered readers, issue after issue, was a record of splendid things achieved and evidence of the validity of things aspired to.

However, what every issue of *Freedomways* made patently clear was that the fight for full citizenship by people of color antedated the turbulence of the Sixties, that it had been unfolding before the electric moment when Rosa Parks refused her seat in the back of the bus and even before the watershed decision of *Brown v. Board*. Before King and Malcolm and Wilkins and Carmichael, and James Farmer, H. Rap Brown, and Fannie Lou Hamer, there had been the Old Left when it was young with its interracialism, its Louis Burnhams and Ben Davises calling for economic empowerment of the poor, its civil libertarian precocity in the first hours of Scottsboro, and its path-breaking Southern Negro Youth Congress.

Many decades after *Freedomways'* opening editorial salvo, the ideals of these iconic personalities have receded from the general consciousness as first the Nixon New Federalism, then the Reagan Revolution, followed by the Clinton Evasion and the Bush Homeland Security State have made the world safe for the Darwinian regime of unregulated capital. Du Bois and Robeson, Baldwin and Hansberry, Julius Nyerere and Ben Davis and John Pittman remain problematic seers in this new order. The sobering, instructive, and politically crucial message of James and Esther Jackson as mediated through *Freedomways* and their splendid collection that now enriches the Tamiment Library reminds us that we would do well to learn to esteem those prophets who are unappreciated in their own country.

Fundamentally Determined: James E. Jackson and Esther Cooper Jackson and the Southern Negro Youth Congress – 1937–1946

JOHNETTA RICHARDS

For most Americans, the civil rights movement is identified with the years 1945 to 1975. Recent scholarship, however, points to a much longer struggle, one which began in the 1930s and in which the Southern Negro Youth Congress (SNYC) played a central role. The SNYC was organized in 1936–7 when black Americans, frustrated by the failure of Franklin D. Roosevelt's New Deal to challenge the southern Jim Crow system of racial segregation began a campaign for civil rights and economic justice. With the New Deal's Agricultural Adjustment Act, which sought to combat agricultural depression by restricting production, forcing African American tenant farmers and sharecroppers off the land, black people began forming tenant farmers unions as they organized "Jobs for Negroes" campaigns. The Communist Party, now in its united front period, and looking to "work with social democratic parties, reformist trade unions and other organizations against class enemies of the proletariat" became an important part of this civil rights and economic justice coalition. This commitment, along with its work with the unemployment councils and anti-lynching campaigns gave the Communist Party (CP) visibility in the black community, even though this only translated into a slight increase in black membership.[1]

Two cases stand out – the Scottsboro Case of 1931 and the Angelo Herndon Case of 1932. In both instances, attorneys sponsored by the CP worked hard for the freedom of these black men and eventually met with some measure of success. This was at a time when most civic organizations turned a blind eye to racism. P.B. Young, an African American reporter with the black southern

---

[1] Georgi Dimitrov, "The Fascist Offensive and the Tasks of the Communist International Struggle of the Working Class Against Fascism," Speech delivered 2 August 1935 before the 7th World Congress of the Communist International, in Dimitrov, *On the United Front* (New Delhi, India: People's Publishing House, 1971), 27.

newspaper, the *Norfolk Journal and Guide* summed up the view of the CP by many black Americans:

> [The CP] is one of the factors in a growing world wide ideal to improve the condition of the underprivileged, to make government more the servant of all the people, to give the rank and file of those who labor a larger share of the fruits of production, and to afford all men equality before the law and equal opportunity to work and live. . . .
>
> The Negro is patriotic and loyal, if he is anything, and communism has gained adherents, and will continue to do so, only because traditional American conditions with race prejudice, economic enslavement, and lack of opportunity, and discrimination of all sorts have made the Negro susceptible to any doctrine, which promises a brighter future, where race and color will not be a penalty.[2]

By the mid-1930s black college students were becoming involved in civil rights activities. James E. Jackson, while attending Virginia Union University in Richmond, Virginia helped start the Cooperative Independent Movement, a club to "train leaders for the deliverance of our people, through militant action, from every semblance of racial and class oppression".[3] This club joined with white students from the University of Virginia to present grievances to the Virginia State Legislature. They protested fascism, war preparations, retrenchment in education and discriminatory hiring practices.

James Jackson, son of a respected pharmacist was well known around Richmond. One of his grade school teachers, Mrs. Edwina Hall, characterized him as polite and pleasant. "He was always sensitive to others' feelings".[4] A Richmond postal worker recalled: "It did not matter to us [James Jackson's CP membership]. We knew he had always tried to help us. We supported him."[5] James E. Jackson appears to have joined the CP by 1931. He worked closely with a number of progressive organizations, including the Cooperative Independent Movement on the campus of Virginia Union, and he was soon to be a founding member of the Southern Negro Youth Congress (SNYC).

The SNYC's inaugural conference was held in Richmond, Virginia on February 13–14, 1937, to coincide with Frederick Douglas' birthday. In an interview, John Edwards, a retired postal worker, remembered his reaction to hearing about the Richmond conference: "We felt that relief was finally on the way. This is going to be a turning point, this Southern Negro Youth Congress.

---

[2]   "Negro Editors on Communism", *Crisis*, April and May 1932, in Herbert Aptheker, ed. *A Documentary History of the Negro People in the United States*, Vol. 3 (Secaucus, New Jersey: Citadel Press, 1977), 701.

[3] Esther Cooper Jackson, "This Is My Husband", pamphlet, National Committee to Defend Negro Leadership, Brooklyn, New York, 1953, 19.

[4] Interview by Johnetta Richards with Edwina Hall, retired school teacher, Virginia Union University, Richmond, Virginia. 2 March 1979.

[5] Interview by Johnetta Richards with John Edwards, retired postal worker, Richmond, Virginia. 14 September 1978.

Many of the people hoped for the Youth Congress. They desperately wanted the congress to effectively work for them." Hosea Hudson, former union organizer, steel worker and Communist Party official recalled: "We black people didn't have no mass organization in the South before then. Nobody said nothin'. Police shoot down a Negro – it just a Negro shot down. Some may have grumbled among themselves, but nobody said nothin'."[6]

With the creation of the Southern Negro Youth Congress, such events would be investigated and publicized to bring about justice. For the first time, southern blacks would have a vehicle to take action and bring about change. Nearly all of the established black civil rights organizations supported the creation of the SNYC in 1937. Even though the NAACP's attitude was somewhat ambivalent because of open communist involvement. However, the SNYC was supported by many black newspapers, prominent clergy, and educational leaders. SNYC's first congress put forth a number of resolutions including: repeal of the poll tax law, universal Negro suffrage, equal treatment before the law, modification of the sharecropping system, economic security and more federal aid to black southerners through public works and school programs.

As he gained recognition for his work with the SNYC, James Jackson was invited by Gunnar Myrdal to become a field investigator on what became the American Dilemma project.[7] While working on this project, he traveled to Nashville, Tennessee and met fellow Virginian and Fisk graduate student Esther Cooper, whom he married in 1941.[8]

Once married, James and Esther Jackson made their home in Birmingham, Alabama where SNYC was then headquartered. Esther became a long-time volunteer with SNYC and eventually joined the staff as organizational secretary. Esther Jackson was born in Arlington, Virginia, where her mother was head of the Arlington chapter of the NAACP. Race activism was part of her consciousness as a young woman well before she entered the university. At one point James or Esther held the position of Secretary, Educational Director, Executive Director and investigators for SNYC. They were involved in most of the organization's activities including the organizing of tobacco workers, creation of the Young Writers and Artists club, and investigation of civil liberties cases.

Organization of Tobacco Workers in Virginia, 1937–1938

The SNYC played a central role in the unionization of Virginia's tobacco stemmers. In 1937, 90% of all black workers in the tobacco industry were stemmers. Wages were based on the weight of the stems removed from the leaves. These workers complained of very low wages, poor ventilation, lack of toilets, lack of dressing rooms, and child labor. The employers even had rules against laughing and talking. One female tobacco worker remembered many

[6] Interview with Hosea Hudson, at his home, Atlantic City, New Jersey, 18 August 1977.
[7] Jackson, "This is My Husband", pamphlet, 24.
[8] *Ibid.*, 26.

FIG. 1. *Cast Your Vote for Youth in 1940*, from the 4th Southern Negro Youth
Conference Registration Packet, New Orleans, April 18–20, 1940.

years later what it was like working as a tobacco stemmer and not being allowed
to go to the bathroom: "There are times in the month you need to go to the
toilet, and sometimes you think you can plan things very nicely, but nature
surprises you, and you need to go to the toilet." One time the blood ran down
her legs "because if you went to the toilet, you would be fired." She said, a male

FIG. 2. Cover, 4th Southern Negro Youth Conference Souvenir Journal, New Orleans, April 18–20, 1940.

co-worker took off his jacket and just wrapped it around her. It was very humiliating and embarrassing. Workers often labored with the windows closed because the foremen wanted to keep the moisture in the tobacco.

The Tobacco Workers International Union (AFL) had begun organizing these workers in 1912. By 1920, 3500 had joined the union, but when conditions did not improve most left. By 1925, there were only about 100 organized

FIG. 3. **Vilma Hopkins, Tobacco Workers' Union leader, June 12, 1947.**
***Daily Worker* photography morgue, reproduced with permission of the**
Communist Party USA.

black tobacco workers in the entire state of Virginia.[9] Viewing the tobacco workers as the most exploited of all workers in Richmond, James Jackson and C. Columbus Alston (CIO) created a plan to organize over 5,000 tobacco stemmers and laborers into the union. During 1938, when representatives of the Export Leaf Factory of the British-American Tobacco Company refused the demands of the black workers, they struck. The factory workers picketed the company for three days carrying signs with their demands: an eight-hour day, time and a half for overtime, toilet facilities, and a halt to child labor. As they marched they sang: "The union is my leader, I shall not be moved."[10] Finally, after a long three-day strike, the employers agreed to their demands.

---

[9] *The Negro in Virginia* (New York: Arno Press, 1969), 308. This book was compiled as part of a project of the Works Progress Administration for the State of Virginia and originally was published by the Virginia Writers Project of the WPA in 1970.

[10] *Ibid.*, 308

Workers in other industries joined the CIO as a result of this campaign. Wiley Hall, Secretary of the Richmond Urban League, described the CIO campaign as "the most significant thing that happened to Richmond Negroes since Emancipation."[11] Eventually seven factories signed union contracts and the income of the black Richmond population increased by $250,000 annually.

Civil Liberties Success — Nora Wilson Case

In 1937 the SNYC moved its headquarters to Birmingham, Alabama, and for the next few years Alabama became the center of its activities. With James Jackson as the Executive Director, the SNYC was at the center of a number of civil liberties cases involving police brutality, intimidation, mob violence, and the southern unequal 'justice' system. The case of Nora Wilson, a black teenage domestic worker from Elmore County, Alabama who was serving time in Wetumpka Women's Prison for using abusive language to a white woman, was the SNYC's first major case. The Caravan Puppeteers brought the plight of Nora Wilson to the attention of the SNYC.

The puppeteers, a black youth group, largely consisting of university students, was sponsored by American Youth Congress and the Southern Negro Youth Congress. They used puppets to both entertain and inform rural southern black people about the movement for the abolition of the poll tax, voter registration drives, and labor unions.[12] They often told the white local officials when seeking permission to perform that they were providing information about dental hygiene, but when the whites left the room the conversation turned to Jim Crow and civil rights. After performing in a number of rural communities during 1940, often using the roof of an old Chevrolet station wagon as a platform, they met Nora Wilson's mother, a black sharecropper and mother of seven children who lived near Millbrook, Alabama. She told the puppeteers that her eldest child, Nora, was serving an eight and one half month sentence in prison for cursing a white woman. At the end of the sentence, Nora was to stand trial for assault and battery with intent to kill.

The indictment of the Grand Jury of the Circuit Court of Elmore County returned 23 August 1940 read:

> State of Alabama vs. Nora Wilson, No. 8850
> Appearing for the State – The Solicitor
> No Attorney for the Defense
>
> Charge: Abusive Language
>
> Disposition: Defendant waives jury... and pleads guilty and is adjudged guilty and is fined $100 and costs. Defendant not paying such fine and cost is

---

[11] *Ibid.*, 309.

[12]"SNYC in the News," Special Edition, *Pittsburg Courier*, "Youth Leader Opens Drive to End Poll Tax". 30 June 1940, Beineke Collection, Yale University, New Haven. Also see Chapter 3, "Activities of the Southern Negro Youth Congress" in the *Southern Negro Youth Congress: A History*, by Johnetta Richards (unpublished Ph.D. diss. University of Cincinnati, 1987).

formerly sentenced to do hard labor for 30 days for fine and 40 days for costs, and six months additional hard labor imposed by court.

Assault with intent to murder
Indictment returned by Grand Jury.[13]

After hearing Mrs. Wilson's story of Nora's imprisonment, members of the Caravan Puppeteers immediately contacted the national office of SNYC in Birmingham, Alabama. James Jackson sent a field representative to investigate the case. Arthur Price, the SNYC representative, learned that Adrien, Nora's eleven year old sister, was accused of stealing six ears of corn while working at the home of neighboring whites. When Nora learned of the accusation she went to the employer, Mrs. Woodburn, who was stunned by the language Nora used as she demanded full pay for the ironing and other work done by her sister. Woodburn slapped Nora for addressing her, a proper southern white woman, in that tone. She also shouted for her husband to bring a gun. Nora ran from the house. It was not long before the sheriff and Mr. Woodburn arrived at the Wilson household with a warrant for the arrest of young Nora Wilson for assault and battery with intent to kill. Nora was immediately arrested with bond set at one thousand dollars. Possible bondholders refused to provide for the "nigger case".[14] Without the benefit of advice from an attorney, friends, or her parents, Nora agreed to waive a jury trial and was convicted and sentenced. Mrs. Woodburn's subsequent request that the sentence be dropped was ignored.

The SNYC launched a campaign to free Nora Wilson after reviewing the report of Arthur Price. James Jackson contacted Malcolm Dobbs of the League of Young Southerners to assist him in the case. After several challenges, Dobbs, who was white, was allowed to visit Nora in the Wetumpka Women's prison. An attorney was retained and the campaign to free Nora Wilson began in earnest. Telegrams, letters and petitions were sent to Alabama's Governor Frank Dixon, and the Justice and Solicitor of Wetumpka, Alabama. Publications produced by SNYC solicited support for Nora and kept readers across the nation informed on her condition. Many of Nora's young friends formed the Millbrook Alabama Negro Youth Council and worked for her freedom.[15] Eventually Nora was released from prison and all charges were dropped before she completed her sentence. The freeing of Nora Wilson greatly encouraged members of the Youth Congress to continue their fights for justice in the South, and outraged many local whites. A supervisor at the Wetumpka Women's prison was quoted as saying: "This is a nigger case and we don't like publicity on these things. Have you anything to do with the Scottsboro case? This case gave us a lot of bad publicity."[16]

---

[13] Jefferson Richards, "Nora Wilson Was Too 'Uppity'...", *The Review*, 5 (December 1940), 11. See Private Papers of Dorothy Burnham and Edward Strong related to SNYC in 1940. Brooklyn, New York.

[14] Augusta V. Jackson, "Free at Last", *Calvalcade*, June 1941, Private Papers of Dorothy Burnham. Brooklyn, New York.

[15] *Ibid.*, Augusta V. Jackson.

[16] Jefferson Richards, *The Review*, 5 (December 1940), 11.

Due to limited resources, the Southern Negro Youth Congress had to limit its involvement in civil liberties cases. However, it organized protests that brought attention to the system of Jim-Crow justice. Petition campaigns, telegrams, letters to the editor, and, where possible, articles in local newspapers often aroused interest and pressured government officials.

Esther Cooper Jackson and FEPC Activities

Esther Cooper was always at the center of SNYC activities. Her role increased significantly when James Jackson was in the army during World War II. Cooper served as an organizer, executive organizational secretary, and editor of SNYC publications. In May 1941, she was part of a delegation selected by SNYC to go to Washington, D.C. to petition the War Department to compel military contractors to hire blacks to work in defense industries. The delegation extended invitations to various representatives to the War Department to address the Fourth of July Mobilization Celebration sponsored by SNYC. With Louis Burnham and Esther Cooper in the lead, members of the delegation included R.R. Pierce of Gee's Bend, Alabama and Mrs. Jewell Mazique of Washington, D.C. Cooper also assisted in the drafting of several letters to the War Department demanding the integration of the armed forces, including ROTC programs, the Air Corps, its training centers, officer candidate schools and the Women's Auxiliary Army Corps.[17]

Initially, their efforts seemed successful. The Fair Employment Practices Commission (FEPC), created by President Roosevelt as a part of Executive Order 8802, held hearings in Birmingham, Alabama in June 1941. As a result, the Alabama State Council of Employment Service and the State Board of Education were ordered to begin immediate training of African American workers for skilled positions in war industries. Technical education classes for African Americans began in Birmingham and Mobile, Alabama. However, by October, training for blacks was halted as the agency claimed that it was impossible for it to find jobs for one hundred earlier graduates of its riveting and chipping training.[18] In response, the SNYC joined with the Birmingham NAACP chapter, the CIO, the AFL and the Urban League in sending protest telegrams to Vice President Henry Wallace, Paul V. McNutt of the Manpower Commission, and Lawrence Craner of the FEPC. These messages stressed the urgency of maintaining and increasing facilities for the continued training of African Americans. The Assistant Executive Secretary of the FEPC, George H. Johnson, responded that the Alabama training program was vital and a full assessment of the situation would take place.

---

[17] SNYC Press Release, 30 October 1942, 2. "Alabama Agencies and Industries Conspire to Bar Negroes from Jobs and Job Training", James Jackson in Private Papers of Dorothy Burnham. Brooklyn, New York.

[18] "Training for Production", n.d., Youth Clippings File, Schomburg Collection, New York, New York. Article by John Beecher, Southern Field Representative for Fair Employment Practices Commission, 1942.

Fɪɢ. 4. **Esther Cooper and Paul Robeson at the Southern Negro Youth Congress, Tuskegee University, Tuskegee, Alabama, 1942.**

At the October 1942 meeting of the SNYC Advisory Board, Esther Cooper stressed that the SNYC needed to mobilize more than ever before for the victory over the Axis Powers and to break all barriers that would impede full participation in the war effort and in attaining full citizenship.[19] With tenacious planning, the SNYC committee sent a resolution to the War Manpower Commission Chief and the Director of the FEPC advocating the expansion of real opportunities for black people. They wanted full implementation of Executive Order 8802 and the complete integration of black workers in all government war plants to win the war.

Association of Young Writers and Artists – Esther Jackson's Project

As the organizational secretary for the SNYC, Esther Cooper spent a good deal of time managing the Association of Young Writers and Artists (AYWA). The prospectus of this association stated the purpose as:

> The long struggle for freedom and citizenship that has been the central aspiration of poets, writers and artists [and in the] day-to-day lives of millions in the cities and on the farms in the South. This ... story that will be written

---

[19]"Committee Plans Fourth of July Rally and Parade," n.d., News article, Edward Strong, Private Papers, New York City, New York.

and sung, painted and dramatized. It is a story that spans 300 years into the past and stretches into the future.[20]

The AYWA held the first quarterly contest during the summer of 1944 with submissions coming from a wide range of colleges including Dillard University, Morgan State, West Virginia State and George Washington school in New York City.[21] Contestants were required to "express in an art form of their choice" their reaction to the novel, *Freedoms' Road* by Howard Fast. A panel headed by Alain Locke selected the winners, Earl Robinson from West Virginia State College and Martha Grover from Morgan State College. Esther Cooper managed this program and provided publicity about the awards.[22] Cooper secured funding from long-time members and the editorial board of AYWA. However, when two grant proposals submitted to the American Missionary Association and the Julius Rosenwald Fund were not funded, the program folded.

Local Advocacy for Black Citizens in Birmingham

As organizational secretary of the SNYC, Esther Cooper threw herself into the struggle to desegregate public accommodations in Birmingham, Alabama. In early 1942 she gathered 6,000 signatures in a petition demanding the integration of the local park and playground on 16th Street in Birmingham.[23] In 1942, Cooper attended a City Council meeting. As she made her presentation to the Birmingham City Council, Commissioner of Public Safety, "Bull" Connor, attempted to prevent her from speaking, but Cooper, very firmly insisted she had a right to address the gathering as she had followed the established protocols. After she submitted her proposal, the council passed a resolution that for the first time allowed black residents to sit on the benches in the park. Though she was successful in this venture, she was careful to refrain from going directly home that night, as "Bull" Connor had vowed to teach her a lesson. Fortunately, no harm came to Cooper as she cleverly avoided her regular routine for several days.[24]

*   *   *   *   *   *

---

[20] News Release, SNYC, 16 February 1944. Private Papers, Dorothy Burnham. Brooklyn, New York; Prospectus of Association of Young Writers and Artists, James Weldon Johnson Papers, Beinecke Collection, Yale University, New Haven, Connecticut.

[21] Letter from Louis Burnham to Arthur Angele, 28 September 1945, Mobile, Alabama. General Correspondence Files, Private Papers of Dorothy Burnham. Brooklyn, New York.

[22] Letter from Mike Ross to Mr. Wilkerson, 17 April 1946. Private Papers of Dorothy Burnham, Brooklyn, New York; Grant Petition of $10,000 to the Robert Marshall Foundation, Finance File, 1947–1948, Private Papers of Dorothy Burnham. Brooklyn, New York.

[23] Interview by Johnetta Richards of Esther Jackson. 13 July 1977 in Jackson home, Brooklyn, New York.

[24] *Ibid.* Interview of Esther Jackson.

During World War II as Esther Cooper provided leadership for the SNYC, James Jackson served with an army engineering battalion on the Burma China frontier. After the war the couple moved to New Orleans and James Jackson became an organizer for the Communist Party and worked closely with the CIO. A series of violent attacks forced Jackson to leave Louisiana. Moving to Detroit James Jackson continued his work for the Communist Party as he organized automobile workers at the Ford River Rouge plant. Cooper went to work for the Civil Rights Congress. Their political careers would continue for nearly 40 more years, however, their SNYC legacy remained fundamental.

The SNYC was the first southern-based black organization to take up the struggle for civil rights during the depression decade. Though its history had mostly been forgotten, it helped lay the foundations of the modern civil rights movement in the south. Under the SNYC's leadership, blacks in rural areas began to understand that they had to organize, vote, and work to advance their political and economic interests. The strategic meetings, involvement of churches, businesses and college students were important parts of the SNYC's legacy that raised the possibility that the South could change, that blacks were entitled to live like any other American citizen. Many of the ideas of continued protest, use of the mass media, educational programs, and non-violent direct action were tools for change that the SNYC used well. Though the SNYC was one of the many casualties of the post-war red scare, Southern black people remembered its accomplishments and this historical memory contributed to the civil rights movement of the 1960s.

Esther V. Cooper's "The Negro Woman Domestic Worker in Relation to Trade Unionism": Black Left Feminism and the Popular Front

ERIK S. McDUFFIE

Esther V. Cooper's brilliant 120-page 1940 M.A. thesis, "The Negro Woman Domestic Worker in Relation to Trade Unionism," still stands as the most thorough sociological and historical study written on the working conditions and status of black women household workers and their efforts to unionize during the Depression.[1] The "Negro Woman Domestic Worker" was a crucial part of her early intellectual foundation, helping to set the stage for her staunch support for civil rights, social justice, internationalism, and radical democracy with special concern for African-American women that were trade marks of her life's work. It also stands as a marker for what could have been a significantly different life journey for her.[2]

---

[1] When discussing her life before her marriage to James E. Jackson in May 1940, I will refer to her as Esther Cooper. Following her marriage, I will refer to her as Esther Cooper Jackson.

[2] Esther V. Cooper, "The Negro Woman Domestics in Relation to Trade Unionism" (M.A. Thesis, Fisk University, 1940); Erik S. McDuffie, "Long Journeys: Four Black Women and the Communist Party, USA, 1930–1956" (unpublished Ph.D. diss., New York University, 2003); Robin D.G. Kelley, *Hammer and Hoe: Alabama Communists During the Great Depression* (Chapel Hill: University of North Carolina Press, 1990), 204; David L. Lewis, *W.E.B. Du Bois: The Fight for Equality* (New York: Henry Holt, 2000).

This article joins a growing body of work focused on black women's encounters with the American Left, see Carole Boyce Davies, *Left of Karl Marx: The Political Life of Black Communist Claudia Jones* (Durham: Duke University Press, 2008); Erik S. McDuffie, "A 'New Freedom Movement of Negro Women': Sojourning for Truth, Justice, and Human Rights during the Early Cold War," *Radical History Review*, 101 (Spring 2008): 81–106; Fanon Che Wilkins, "Beyond Bandung: The Critical Nationalism of Lorraine Hansberry, 1950–1965," *Radical History Review*, 95 (2006): 191–210; Jacqueline Ann Castledine, "Gendering the Cold War: Race, Class and Women's Peace Politics, 1945–1975" (unpublished PhD diss., Rutgers University, 2006); Erik S. McDuffie, "'[She] devoted twenty minutes condemning all other forms of government but the Soviet': Black Women Radicals in the Garvey Movement and in the Left during the 1920s" in *Diasporic Africa: A Reader*, Michael A. Gomez, ed., (New York: New York University Press, 2006), 219–250; Dayo Falayon Gore, "To Hold a Candle in the Wind: Black Women Radicals and Post-World War II U.S. Politics" (unpublished PhD diss.,

The thesis, above all, contains broad significance for understanding black women's activism and black radicalism during the Popular Front. It reveals an emergent black left feminism, a politics that centers working-class women by combining Communist Party positions on race, gender, and class with black nationalism and black radical women's lived experiences, embedded in their writings and activism. Black left feminism paid special attention to the intersectional, transnational nature of African-American women's oppression and viewed them as key agents for transformative change. Committed to the Popular Front agenda of civil rights, trade unionism, anti-fascism, internationalism, and concern for women's equality, their work anticipating conclusions drawn by "second wave" black feminism decades later.[3]

The initial idea for the thesis stemmed from Cooper's observations as an undergraduate at Oberlin College of African-American women who cooked and cleaned the school's dormitories and then returned home late at night to a small ghetto in town. "They had little future and no union," Cooper Jackson recalled. Her interest in their plight was further bolstered during her years as a graduate student in the Masters program in Sociology at Fisk University in Nashville, Tennessee. Her graduate fellowship required her to work at a settlement house in a poor black neighborhood near Fisk's campus. The experience opened her eyes to black urban, southern poverty. Many of her impoverished clients were black women who worked back-breaking days in the homes of wealthy white people. She approached her advisor, white economist Dr. Addison Cutler, about writing a thesis on black women domestics, and he gave his enthusiastic support for the project. Dr. Charles Johnson,

---

(footnote continued)
New York University, 2003); Mary Helen Washington, "Alice Childress, Lorraine Hansberry, and Claudia Jones: Black Women Write the Popular Front," in *Left of the Color Line: Race, Radicalism, and Twentieth Century Literature of the United States*, ed. Bill V. Mullen and James Smethurst (Chapel Hill: University of North Carolina Press, 2003), 183–204; Kate Weigand, *Red Feminism: American Communism and the Making of Women's Liberation* (Baltimore: Johns Hopkins University Press, 2001), 97–113; Gerald Home, *Race Woman: The Lives of Shirley Graham Du Bois* (New York: New York University Press, 2000).

[3] The term "black left feminism" is borrowed from Washington, "Black Women Write the Popular Front," 185, 193–198.

Cooper was a child of the Popular Front. Her interest in trade unionism, civil rights, and global affairs, which set the stage for her decision to write her master's thesis on African-American women domestic workers, began while she attended Oberlin College and blossomed as a graduate student in sociology at Fisk University during the late 1930s. She attended school at one of the most dynamic moments in college protests in the U.S. prior to the 1960s. The Spanish Civil War, labor upheaval, and U.S. intervention in World War II generated passionate debates and vibrant student movements at Oberlin, capturing Cooper's attention and imagination. At Fisk, she quickly gravitated towards a group of left-wing professors, many of whom were white. They invited her to join a reading group held in what she described as an "Anne Frank-like room," introducing her to the writings of Marx and Lenin. It was at one of these meetings when one of her professors in the presence of her advisor signed her up in the Communist Party. McDuffie, "Long Journeys," 63–71, 284–294; Kelley, *Hammer and Hoe*, 205; Robert Cohen, *When the Old Left Was Young: Student Radicals and America's First Mass Student Movement, 1929–1941* (New York: Oxford University Press, 1993), 207–208.

the prominent black sociologist and former head of the Urban League who was now on the faculty at Fisk, also strongly supported her thesis.[4]

The methodology of "The Negro Woman Domestic Worker" was distinguished by Cooper's creative use of sources that brought to life the miserable conditions in which black women household laborers toiled and their agency in fighting for a better future. She cited U.S. Labor Department, CIO and AFL reports, census, and samples of union contracts that covered about 2,000 of the nearly 600,000 African-American women nationally who toiled as domestic workers. She used comparative data on domestic labor unions from Scandinavia, the Soviet Union, pre-fascist Italy, and other countries. Above all, she interviewed and spoke with dozens of black women household workers in New York, Newark, Chicago, and Washington, DC, giving them a voice and recognizing them as key agents in their fight for freedom, dignity, and respect.[5]

The thesis' main argument contended "the problems faced by Negro women domestic workers are responsive to amelioration through trade union organizations."[6] She rejected the mainstream American labor movement's position that domestic and agricultural workers, and white-collar professionals were "unorganizable." Such claims "have been proven false," she argued, by the success in organizing household laborers in Western Europe and, above all, the Soviet Union. In stark contrast to the U.S., she pointed out that in the U.S.S.R. "the social standing of domestic workers is equal to any other worker."[7] Clearly, Cooper saw advances made for household laborers in the Soviet Union as a model for improving the lives and status of laboring black women in particular and American workers generally.

The thesis detailed the highly exploitative nature of domestic labor. Cooper called attention to the "social stigma" of domestic work, noting that the relationship between employer and African-American female household workers "exhibited all the characteristics of the feudal relationship of master and serf." Black women domestic workers "have been discriminated against and exploited with double harshness." She cited long-hours, low wages, poor work conditions, lack of job security, mainstream labor's neglect of domestic workers, absent job standards, the isolating nature of household labor, and the exemption of domestics from old age insurance and unemployment benefits under the 1935 Social Security Act as major obstacles that black women domestics encountered.[8]

Some of the thesis' most insightful discussions concerned the ways in which race, gender, and class not only positioned black female domestic workers at the

---

[4] McDuffie, 295–296.

[5] Cooper, 99; McDuffie, 296–297.

[6] For discussions of the gendered implications of and the exclusion of domestics, migrant farm laborers, and other occupations from receiving benefits and protections under the 1935 Social Security Act, see Linda Gordon, *Pitied But Not Entitled: Single Mothers and the History of Welfare* (Cambridge: Harvard University Press, 1994), 4–6, 253–263, 293–297; Michael B. Katz, *In the Shadow of the Poorhouse: A Social History of Welfare in America*, rev. ed. (New York: Basic Books, 1996), 242–252.

[7] Cooper, 27, 29, 30.

[8] *Ibid.*, 3, 6.

bottom of the economic ladder but provided white women with some freedom from performing tedious, back-breaking household work. She singled out the infamous Bronx "slave market," street corners in the borough where black women stood waiting to be hired for day labor by white housewives, as "[o]ne of the worst types of human exploitation ... found in New York City, and one of its ugliest aspects is the way in which girls are shipped up in car loads from the South to stand on corners waiting for work at 25 to 35 cents per hour." She wrote: "Housewives, knowing they can get domestic workers at almost starvation wages have played employee against employee."[9] By calling attention to the Bronx slave market, Cooper illustrated the ways in which white and black women were divided along race and class lines. She in effect rejected the notion that "woman" was a universal, ahistorical category, directly challenging ideas posited by some white Communist women theoreticians at this time that women were equally oppressed by patriarchy.[10]

Despite these obstacles in organizing black women domestic workers, Cooper was still optimistic about their future. She cited Section 7a of the 1933 National Industrial Recovery Act and the 1935 National Labor Relations Act as important new opportunities for allowing organized labor to expand its ranks. She praised the African-American women-led Domestic Workers Union for its trailblazing work in unionizing black women household workers and lauded the CIO for its "conviction ... that unionization is possible for domestic workers."[11] In this respect, the CIO and domestic worker unions signified immense possibilities for not only improving the lot of African-American female wage-earners but in bringing them into the heart of the American labor movement. In doing so, her argument implicitly suggested that the unionization of black female domestics would benefit the entire American labor movement.[12]

Cooper's "The Negro Woman Domestic Worker" was a part of a larger discussion in politically progressive black women's circles and in the African-American community generally about the plight of female household workers. Black periodicals during these years were filled with probing articles on the subject.[13]

The most famous was the 1938 muck-raking exposé, "The Bronx Slave Market," published in the *Crisis* magazine by Ella Baker and Marvel Cooke. The article discussed the humiliating, exploitative realities encountered daily by black women desperately in search of work and income. "Rain or shine, cold or hot," they wrote, "you will find them there—Negro women, old and young—sometimes bedraggled sometimes neatly dressed—but with the invariable paper bundle, waiting expectantly for Bronx housewives to buy their strength and energy for an hour, two hours, or even for a day at the munificent rate of fifteen,

---

[9] *Ibid.*, 98.

[10] Margaret Cowl, *Women and Equality* (New York: Workers Library, 1935), 3; McDuffie, 256.

[11] Cooper, 104, 31–97.

[12] McDuffie, 300–301; Cooper, 98–105.

[13] Mary Anderson, "The Plight of Negro Domestic Labor," *The Journal of Negro Education* 5 (January 1936): 66–72; *Amsterdam News*, 16 October 1937, 13, 19; Cooper, v–x.

FIG. 1. Domestic workers on strike, New York City, 1942. *Daily Worker* **photography morgue, reproduced with permission of the Communist Party USA.**

twenty, or, if luck be with them, thirty cents an hour." Both Baker and Cooke had ties to the Left. The former associated with an eclectic crowd of Harlem and downtown radicals while the latter joined the Communist Party but kept her membership in it private.[14]

Louise Thompson's important 1936 essay, "Toward a Brighter Dawn," published in the CPUSA-affiliated *Woman Today* magazine, posited ground-breaking analysis about the plight of African-American women domestics that anticipated modern black feminism. Like Cooper, Thompson paid special attention to the Bronx "slave market," declaring that it represented "a graphic monument to this most exploited section of the American working class population—the Negro Woman. Over the whole land, Negro women meet this triple exploitation—as workers, as women, and as Negroes." They constituted, therefore, "the most exploited group in America." Similar to Cooper's thesis, Thompson vocally supported the unionization of household workers, and she credited the National Negro Congress for its support of these campaigns.[15] It was this call coupled with their left-wing sympathies for more radical approaches to addressing racial inequalities, economic disparities, and the marginal status of black women that distinguished the writings of Esther

---

[14] Ella Baker and Marvel Cooke, "The Bronx Slave Market," *Crisis* 42 (November 1935): 330–331, 340; Marvel Cooke, interview with author, 1 April 1998, 11 June 1998, New York, NY; Barbara J. Ransby, *Ella Baker and the Black Freedom Movement: A Radical Democratic Vision* (Chapel Hill: University of North Carolina Press, 2003), 76–78, 79; Rodger Streitmatter and Barbara Diggs-Brown, "Marvel Cooke: An African-American Woman Journalist Who Agitated for Racial Reform," *Afro-Americans in New York Life and History* 16 (July 1992), 57–58; *Philadelphia Inquirer*, 22 February 1998, HI, H8.

[15] Louise Thompson, "Toward a Brighter Future," *The Woman Today* (April 1936): 14, 30.

Cooper, Marvel Cooke, Ella Baker, and Louise Thompson from more politically mainstream discussions of household laborers.

Cooper completed her thesis in the spring of 1940, and it caught the attention of renowned sociologist Robert Park, who offered her a fellowship to work on her Ph.D. under his direction at the University of Chicago. Cooper, however, turned it down and opted instead to work for the Southern Negro Youth Congress in Birmingham. She intended to complete her graduate studies one day but she got "busy organizing in the south." The chance to organize in the South and to materialize her commitment to racial justice and democracy was for Cooper just too good an opportunity to pass up. To be sure, Cooper never abandoned her interest in writing and intellectual analysis as best evidenced in co-founding and serving as editor of *Freedomways* magazine that creatively bridged politics, culture, and activism for a quarter century. In this light, her thesis stands as an important early development in the making of a black radical activist intellectual who helped usher in the modern Civil Rights Movement.[16]

In addition, Cooper's thesis along with the writing and activism of black women on the Left foreshadowed arguments made by black Communist leader, theoretician Claudia Jones after World War II that black laboring women constituted the most exploited segment in the African-American community and in the U.S. working-class. Black women, not industrial white workers therefore represented the vanguard of the working-class. This argument in effect turned orthodox Marxism and traditional approaches to labor organizing on their heads, suggesting radically new ways in which to theorize race, gender, class, and politics and to promote social change—ideas that were further developed after the late 1960s by the Third World Women's Alliance, Combahee River Collective, Angela Davis, and bell hooks, amongst others.[17]

Finally, many of the observations and conclusions drawn in "The Negro Woman Domestic Worker" are as relevant today as they were 60 years ago. African-American women are still arguably the most exploited group in the U.S. and disproportionately located in low-paying, low-status, non-unionized service industries. Black women earn 68.4 cents to every dollar earned by a white man. Nearly one-quarter of all African-American women live below the

---

[16] Della Scott, "An Interview with Esther Jackson," *Abafazi: The Simmons College Journal of Women of African Descent* 9, 1 (Fall/Winter 1998), 4; Kelley, 205.

[17] Claudia Jones, "An End to the Neglect of the Problems of the Negro Woman!" *Political Affairs* 28, 6 (June 1949): 51–67; McDuffie; Washington, 183–204; Barbara J. Ransby, *Ella J. Baker and the Black Freedom Movement: A Radical Democratic Vision* (Chapel Hill: University of North Carolina Press, 2003); Daniel Horowitz, *Betty Friedan and the Making of The Feminine Mystique: The American Left, the Cold War, and Modern Feminism* (Amherst: University of Massachusetts Press, 1998); Kimberly Springer, *Living for the Revolution: Black Feminist Organizations, 1968–1980* (Durham, NC: Duke University Press, 2005); Stephen Ward, "The Third World Women's Alliance: Black Feminist Radicalism and Black Power Politics," in *The Black Power Movement: Rethinking the Civil Rights – Black Power Era*, ed. Peniel E. Joseph (New York: Routledge, 2006), 119–144; Benita Roth, *Separate Roads to Feminism: Black, Chicana, and White Feminist Movements in America's Second Wave* (Cambridge: Cambridge University Press, 2004); Premilla Nadasen, *Welfare Warriors: The Welfare Rights Movement in the United States* (New York: Routledge, 2005).

poverty line. The unemployment rate of black women is 9.5%, almost double the national average and nearly 60% higher than that of white women. And African-American women make up one of the fastest growing populations in the prison industrial complex.[18]

Many of the challenges in unionizing black women today are also the same ones that confronted organizers in the 1930s. At the same time, there are new realities in this era of neo-liberalism and corporate globalization, increased migrations of African-descended people from the Caribbean and Africa, and anxiety generated by the "war on terror" for those committed to expansive visions of democracy. "The Negro Woman Domestic Worker," therefore, can help put these present-day struggles into a broader historical perspective.

---

[18] Amy Caiazza, April Shaw, and Misha Werchkul, "The Status of Women in the States, Women's Economic Status in the States: Wide Disparities by Race, Ethnicity, and Religion," Institute for Women's Policy Research, www.iwpr.org, 27; http://www.dol.gov/wb/factsheets/Of-ESWM05.htm; Joy James, ed., *The Angela Davis Reader* (Maiden, MA: Blackwell Publishers, 1998), 60–107.

"All those rosy dreams we cherish": James Jackson and Esther Cooper's Marriage on the Front Lines of the Double Victory Campaign

SARA E. RZESZUTEK

June 16, 1945 was a dull, hot, and sticky day along the Ledo Road in Burma. Corporal James E. Jackson, Jr. sat down in his barrack to write a letter to his wife in Birmingham, Alabama. Several pages passed as Jackson commented on the Communist Party, USA's debate over whether to expel Earl Browder for suggesting that communism and capitalism could peacefully coexist. Then, in a moment of self-reflection, Jackson realized that his letter might not offer his wife the affection she might need to sustain her romantic interest while he was overseas. Jackson did typically write political letters, and it was not uncommon for him to receive similar political letters from his wife. Still, he found humor in the nature of his marriage. Did his wife ever just wish he would send her a flowery note, free from the world's drama, he wondered. "Politics, politics, politics!!!" Jackson joked, "'What a lover,' you must say, 'he quotes Marx on the class struggle and other girls get Keats and Shelley and Browning on June Moon's and stuff...Whatta dope!' (Smiles!)"[1]

When Esther Cooper, Jackson's wife, received the letter, she was probably too busy to have spent much time on poetry.[2] Cooper was serving as the Executive Secretary of the Southern Negro Youth Congress (SNYC), a left-wing organization dedicated to fighting white supremacy in the South. Her busy position entailed endless committee meetings, travel, investigations, budgeting, publishing organizational materials, and keeping up with the many SNYC councils and affiliate groups throughout the South, all for very little money. In the midst of political discussion, consideration of an application for a Rosenwald fellowship, reporting on a new Alabama law to force prospective voters to interpret the Constitution, and an update on their daughter, Harriet

---

[1] James Jackson (JJ) to Esther Cooper (EC), 16 June 1945. James and Esther Cooper Jackson Papers, Tamiment Library, New York University, New York City, hereafter referred to as Jackson Papers.
[2] Esther Cooper kept her maiden name until 1951.

Dolores, Cooper found a moment to reply to her husband's kidding. Cooper wrote, "Yes, I do like Shelley, Browning, and Keats like other girls but please don't slow up on the politics. I'd rather discuss everything with you than anyone in the world."[3] In World War II, the combination of politics and romance was integral to sustaining Cooper and Jackson's relationship over time and distance.

There was an interplay of love and activism in Cooper and Jackson's marriage during the World War II years. The way Cooper and Jackson interpreted, cultivated, and maneuvered through the intersections of personal and political life during World War II sheds light on how larger political changes affected individuals and families, and ultimately helps to explain the ways in which the Black Freedom Movement adapted to a changing world. Southern Negro Youth Congress work, Army service, and Popular Front activism were infused in the couple's family life. As they gained exposure to a wider world in conflict and as their family grew, Cooper and Jackson's personal and political priorities matured and their activism and relationship reflected their wartime experiences. During the war, Cooper and Jackson prepared for a postwar life together where they could continue to be active in mainstream civil rights work while retaining their Popular Front ideology. The way Cooper and Jackson imagined their future during World War II helped them to carve out individual niches in the Black Freedom Movement without compromising their ideological integrity.

During World War II, Cooper and Jackson worked for the SNYC, the latter as Educational Director. In 1937, James Jackson and other young radicals founded the SNYC because they believed that an organization administered in the South by young black Southerners would have a unique advantage in uniting black and white youth against Jim Crow segregation. In 1939, the organization moved its headquarters from Richmond, Virginia to Birmingham, Alabama. Despite its name, the SNYC was open to like-minded activists of all ages, races, and regions.

The SNYC consistently fused a pragmatic, grassroots agenda—basic improvements in everyday conditions for black Southerners—with a broad ideological and international program. The organization was engaged in voter registration and anti-lynching campaigns, efforts to improve education and health care for black Southerners, and unionization drives. Simultaneously, SNYC leaders participated in a large international network of radical youth organizations. As a Popular Front organization, the SNYC was influenced by but not tied to Communist ideology.[4] The organization worked closely with mainstream activist leaders even though it was leftist in its political

---

[3] EC to JJ, 28 June 1945, Jackson Papers.

[4] In 1935, the Communist International initiated a movement that became known as the Popular Front. The Popular Front reflected a move away from the sectarian, forceful Party line. The goal of the Popular Front movement was to unite leftist organizations and quietly influence activism across the world with Communist ideas. Communists joined a wide network of labor unions, civil rights organizations, and any other group that explicitly opposed fascism. Instead of forcing these organizations to adopt strict Communism, these organizations were subtly influenced by the ideas, suggestions, and methods advocated by the Party members. Between 1936 and 1938, the CPUSA doubled its

orientation, which permitted it to straddle the ideological line between radical and realistic progress. The SNYC had the support of prominent black academics, activists, politicians, and professionals.[5] In the SNYC, Cooper and Jackson found a vehicle for change and place to anchor their political goals.

Drafted into the Army in 1943, Jackson left his wife and infant daughter, Harriet Dolores, in Birmingham. He went overseas excited about the opportunity to defend democracy against fascism. The couple reunited in February 1946. Roughly twelve hundred pages of World War II letters between them comprise the basis for understanding how Cooper and Jackson developed their views about national and international politics, their strategies for the black freedom struggle in the South, their ideas about marriage, and how all of this was linked.[6]

Because Cooper and Jackson were only married for about two busy years before Jackson was drafted into the Army, the pair crafted their radical political marriage largely through correspondence during the three-year period of separation. During these years, Cooper was able to thoroughly cultivate her independence within her marriage, and assert herself against the common assumption that a woman would have to choose between her career and her love. Over the same time, Jackson had the opportunity to reconcile any internalized expectations he held for a traditional marriage with both his deep belief in female equality and the pride he took in his wife's career and ambition. The couple used the context of war to define their marriage alongside their increased exposure to internationalism and Southern Negro Youth Congress activism on the home front.

Cooper and Jackson maintained a strong and open relationship during their time apart. After discussing marriage with her sister, Kat, whose husband was also serving overseas, Cooper was stunned to hear how much her sister and brother-in-law kept from each other. They feared sharing their secrets and worries because they believed it would hurt the other's morale. Cooper expressed relief that she and her husband had such an open line of communication, and wrote to Jackson, "I'm so happy we don't believe in

---

(*footnote continued*)

membership. It is important to note that many of the Communist influenced organizations, Civil Rights oriented or otherwise, were interracial and working-class. See Ellen Schrecker, *Many Are the Crimes: McCarthyism in America* (Boston: Little, Brown, & Company, 1998), 15.

[5] Augusta Jackson Strong, "Southern Youth's Proud Heritage," *Freedomways Magazine*, No. 1, 1964, 36; Augusta V. Jackson, "A New Deal for Tobacco Workers," *The Crisis*, October, 1938, 322–324, 330, 324; Esther Cooper Jackson interviews with author; Robin D.G. Kelley, *Hammer and Hoe: Alabama Communists During the Great Depression* (Chapel Hill: University of North Carolina Press, 1990); Patricia Sullivan, *Days of Hope: Race and Democracy in the New Deal Era* (Chapel Hill: University of North Carolina Press, 1996); Johnetta Richards, "The Southern Negro Youth Congress: A History," (unpublished Ph.D. diss., University of Ohio, 1987).

[6] Esther Cooper Jackson and James Jackson, interviews with Sara Rzeszutek, 2002–2006; Erik S. McDuffie, "Long Journeys: Four Black Women and the Communist Party, U.S.A., 1930–1956," (unpublished Ph.D. diss., New York University, 2003); Sarah Hart Brown, "Esther Cooper Jackson: A Life in the Whirlwind" in Bruce L. Clayton and John A. Salmond, eds., *"Lives Full of Struggle and Triumph": Southern Women, Their Institutions, and Their Communities* (Gainesville: University of Florida Press, 2003); Robin D.G. Kelley, *Hammer and Hoe*.

that prevalent idea about sheltering each other from our problems...I'm not only your wife, but your best friend and companion. And darling—if you disagree with anything I've said or done—tell me always. Our marriage must serve as an 'example' to all our friends, relatives, and the youth of the South."[7] Cooper and Jackson understood that their relationship was connected to their politics, and that activists should be sure to embody their politics in their personal lives. They believed that the example of marriage and gender relations they offered was connected to the more straightforward political advances the SNYC fought to achieve.

Cooper and Jackson's marriage was unique in many regards. Historians have offered substantial analysis of marriage in the twentieth century, examining issues like patriarchy, divorce, race, and class. Much of the work on married life examines the gaps between the perception of domestic bliss and the reality of the work that goes into maintaining a household. In the dominant model, women, despite their efforts at asserting autonomy, are either victims of patriarchy or their marriage fails.[8] For many married couples, black or white, equal relations in marriage meant sacrificing power and not performing normative gender roles, and performing traditional gender roles meant inequality between partners.

The historian Martin Summers notes that some black couples deviated from the traditional model of gender relations in marriage during the Harlem Renaissance. Focusing on Wallace Thurman and Louise Thompson, Zora Neale Hurston and Herbert Sheen, and Paul and Eslanda Goode Robeson, Summers suggests a changing outlook on marriage during the 1920s. According to Summers, these three couples represented an experiment with the idea of "modern marriage" among black couples in the 1920s. During this period, Summers argues, "Marriage was no longer solely defined as a union between a man and a woman for the purpose of starting a family that would, in turn, fit into a larger social network. Rather, marriage was becoming more of a means through which to experience individual self-fulfillment."[9] In all three of these unions, however, the couples became discontented and either divorced or led entirely separate private and public lives.

For black couples, a breaking from the traditional model of marriage was different than it was for white couples. Because the legacies of slavery attached increased historical meaning to marriage for black Americans, many fought

---

[7] EC to JJ, 2 July 1945, Jackson Papers.

[8] Works on 20th century marriage include Elaine Tyler May, *Great Expectations: Marriage & Divorce in Post-Victorian America* (Chicago: University of Chicago Press, 1980); Nancy Cott, *Public Vows: A History of Marriage and the Nation* (Cambridge: Harvard University Press, 2000). Works focusing more explicitly on race include Anastasia Curwood, "Three African American Marriages in the World of E. Franklin Frazier, 1932–1967," (unpublished Ph.D. diss., Princeton University, 2003); Eleanor Alexander, *Lyrics of Sunshine and Shadow: The Tragic Courtship and Marriage of Paul Laurence Dunbar and Alice Ruth Moore, A History of Love and Violence among the African American Elite* (New York: New York University Press, 2001).

[9] Martin Summers, *Manliness and its Discontents: The Black Middle Class and the Transformation of Masculinity, 1900–1930* (Chapel Hill: University of North Carolina Press, 2004), 187.

hard since Reconstruction to follow the white middle class model of marriage—husbands working and supporting, wives enjoying the domesticity that they were denied during slavery. Black couples whose gender expression deviated from tradition were engaged with a different marital discourse than white couples who did the same. For black couples, there was an added pressure to defy stereotypes and prove themselves successful at normative models of marriage. This aspiration is predominantly associated with black couples who either had or sought to attain middle class status.[10] Black and white couples who experimented with gender roles in their marriage may have been aspiring to the same egalitarian ideal, but for black couples, this move resonated with a long history of invalidated relationships and the exploitation of male and female labor.

Still, Cooper and Jackson's marriage was not a total historical anomaly. Others in Cooper and Jackson's SNYC cohort had similar relationships. Ed and Augusta Strong and Louis and Dorothy Burnham also practiced the same sort of gender egalitarianism as Cooper and Jackson.[11] For communists like Cooper and Jackson, fundamentally restructuring the economic system in the United States took priority over attaining a bourgeois ideal. They did not seek to create a black middle class as a parallel to the white middle class through their roles within their marriage; instead, they believed that racial equality needed to be attained through more sweeping change. The couple believed that inherent in the emergence of a new economic system would be the transformation of gender relations in public and private life. Cooper and Jackson's gender and class politics, and, accordingly, their marriage, were vital to their activism against racism.

The comfort of Cooper and Jackson's egalitarian and honest relationship was crucial to easing the psychological trauma of war. On May 4, 1945, Jackson described a particularly gruesome scene which resulted in the death of a soldier who "couldn't understand why and for what [he was dying] and he needed more time to learn such things: how to die like a hero for a cause."[12] Jackson, clearly shaken, wrote to Cooper, "Such a day leaves one weary and sick of all the blood and broken flesh and pallid faces... and then your letters come like a mountain breeze quaffing the dead leaves away and leaving the bright green blades swaying in the sunlight... together we shall triumph over every hardship and forlorn mood and no matter what tomorrow brings—it will be good because you love me."[13] This experience illustrated for Jackson just how

---

[10] Eric Foner, *Reconstruction: America's Unfinished Revolution, 1863–1877* (New York: Harper and Row Publishers, 1988); Jacqueline Jones, *Labor of Love, Labor of Sorrow: Black Women, Work and the Family, from Slavery to the Present* (New York: Vintage Books, 1985); Michele Mitchell, *Righteous Propagation: African Americans and the Politics of Racial Destiny after Reconstruction* (Chapel Hill: University of North Carolina Press, 2004); Kevin K. Gaines, *Uplifting the Race: Black Leadership, Politics, and Culture in the Twentieth Century* (Chapel Hill: University of North Carolina Press, 1995).

[11] Kelley, *Hammer and Hoe: Alabama Communists During the Great Depression* (Chapel Hill: University of North Carolina Press, 1990).

[12] JJ to EC, 4 May 1945, Jackson Papers.

[13] *Ibid.*

thoroughly important his marriage was in maintaining his stability through the war. It also led him to reflect on the problem of infidelity while husbands were overseas. Jackson argued that women who were unfaithful were "performing a service to the enemy. One such case can undermine the spirit of a whole battalion for the one reward every soldier expects is for 'his girl' to remain 'true' to him."[14] For Jackson, love and the stability of his marriage were not only personally important, but critical to wartime victory as well.

For Cooper and Jackson, their love and commitment were fundamentally connected to both building morale and formulating political strategies. World War II allowed for a tremendous fluidity of political ideologies for black activists. The Black Freedom Movement in the war years was rooted in both the desire to defeat fascism and a desperate need to address the contradictions of fighting fascism with a segregated army, workforce, and homeland. Historians have addressed the multifaceted layers of black activism and leadership during World War II and have shown that protest activities—either through organizations or on an individual basis—ranged from using the framework of the federal government to employ workers to "everyday resistance" to rioting.[15] Cooper and Jackson would often vent their disgust with racism in the United States and in the Army, and then use the letters as a place to convert their outrage into productive energy.

Outside of writing letters to editors and his wife, there was little Jackson could contribute to the struggles in the South from the Ledo Road, an area which was isolated from much of the world and even from the rest of the war. The China-Burma-India (CBI) Theater of war was not as immediate a priority as the European Theater of Operations or the Pacific Theater of Operations. It started as a Lend-Lease project to assist in building roads to transport equipment across remote areas. Over 60 percent of the engineers sent to the CBI were black. By late 1944, when Jackson arrived, the purpose of the CBI Theater was to keep Japanese attention divided.[16] Jackson worked as a pharmacist with the 823rd Engineering Battalion, and his unit rarely saw much of the action that

---

[14] JJ to EC, 26 April 1945, Jackson Papers.

[15] Herbert Garfinkel, *When Negroes March: The March on Washington Movement in the Organizational Politics for the FEPC* (Glencoe: The Free Press, 1959); Richard M. Dalfiume, "The Forgotten Years of the Negro Revolution," *Journal of American History*, 55 (1968) 90–106; Neil A. Wynn, *The Afro-American and the Second World War* (New York: Holmes & Meier Publishers, Inc., 1975, 1993); Ronald Takaki, *Double Victory: A Multicultural History of America in World War II* (Boston: Little, Brown and Company, 2000); David Levering Lewis, *W.E.B. Du Bois: The Fight for Equality and the American Century, 1919–1963* (New York: Henry Holt and Company, 2000); Patricia Sullivan, *Days of Hope: Race and Democracy in the New Deal Era* (Chapel Hill: University of North Carolina Press, 1996); Robin D.G. Kelley, *Race Rebels: Culture, Politics, and the Black Working Class* (New York: The Free Press, 1994); George Lipsitz, "Frantic to Join . . . the Japanese Army: Black Soldiers and Civilians confront the Asia Pacific War," in T. Fujitani, Geoffrey M. White, and Lisa Yoneyama, eds. *Perilous Memories: the Asia-Pacific War(s)* (Durham: Duke University Press, 2001); Jacquelyn Down Hall, "The Long Civil Rights Movement and the Political Uses of the Past," *Journal of American History*, March 2005, http://www.historycooperative.org/journals/jah/91.4/hall.html, 29 Apr 2006.

[16] Charles F. Romanus and Riley Sunderland, *United States Army in World War II, China-Burma-India Theater: Time Runs out in CBI* (Washington, DC: Office of the Chief of Military History, Department of the Army, 1959), 291.

FIG. 1. James E. Jackson, Jr. in the U.S. Army, Ledo Road, Burma, 1943.

any of the combat units might have seen in the CBI. In fact, by March 1945, only a couple of months after Jackson arrived, a military victory at Lashio meant that the Burma-India section of the Theater had accomplished the most important of its combat goals. The Burma-India section subsequently focused its resources on offering "logistical support" to the China and Southeast Asian Theaters.[17] Many of the injuries Jackson witnessed, then, were caused by equipment malfunctions, or were the result of incidents that the 823rd encountered, but did not participate in. Nonetheless, the area was still very dangerous.

As much as Jackson was excited to participate in a war to save democracy, he felt stifled in this context. He wanted to produce real progress toward democracy, and once drafted, World War II seemed like an ideal way to make a broad contribution to international justice. Instead, the dizzying heat, torrential rain, and "picayune" commanders on the Ledo Road made him want to "consign the army and all of its components to a choice spot in hell."[18] Jackson's heart was on the front lines of the black freedom movement in the U.S. South. Even though he looked forward to telling "Junior," the son he and his wife hoped for upon his return, about "how I won the war," he could not produce real democracy in his immediate surroundings, let alone the whole world.[19] Jackson was not the kind of man who worked well behind the scenes, and he regularly offered suggestions to the SNYC leadership through his

[17] *Ibid.*
[18] JJ to EC, 5 February 1945, Jackson Papers.
[19] JJ to EC, 10 February 1945, *Ibid.*

correspondence with his wife.[20] On the Ledo Road, Jackson needed Cooper not only to build his morale by making him feel loved, but also to help him feel like he was making real contributions to real struggles at home. Cooper knew that Jackson's suggestions for the SNYC were not only beneficial to the organization, but also crucial to his morale. Jackson's marriage to Cooper allowed him to stay engaged in the fight at home, as the SNYC became a vehicle for the couple's political expression and a site where the couple could bond over a common experience.

Cooper and Jackson's relationship with each other and their roles in the SNYC allowed them to use their correspondence as a productive space. Jackson often vented his personal frustrations with segregation in the South and the military with his wife in ways that he certainly would not have in formal settings. Military life was extremely frustrating for black soldiers like Jackson, and the insults of segregation took their toll. The contradiction of fighting a war for democracy with a segregated Army reinforced the urgency of SNYC work for the couple. Both partners used their correspondence to air their uncensored disgust with the South in the confines of their relationship and then move forward, generating broad strategies for change through discussion of SNYC activities and plans.

In one instance, Jackson told his wife about an aquatic training session at a white camp near the Tuskegee Air Force Base, where part of his training took place. Jackson's unit ate dinner at the camp, where "it was jim crow from 'soup to nuts.'"[21] After describing the rigid segregation patterns at the camp, Jackson continued:

> Damned little cracker imbeciles were stationed everywhere to see that we sat apart from the white soldiers...Southern bigots, everyone. Enforcing their jim crow pattern like they were commissioned by God to do so... I have never really known the full measure of my hatred for the South and its native fascist way of life until I came here.[22]

Jackson, who grew up in Richmond, Virginia and had also lived in Birmingham, Alabama, was no stranger to segregation. However, the enthusiasm the white Southerners expressed in maintaining racial separation while waging a war against fascism fueled Jackson's disgust.

Had Jackson published an anecdote about this incident in an SNYC newsletter, for instance, he surely would have told the story differently. While he would not have masked the insult of segregation, he most certainly would have excised terms like "cracker" and suppressed his own personal revulsion. The way that he described this incident to his wife, however, demonstrates that even black activists who were polished, courageous, and devoted to their cause still had thoroughly human responses to the pure offensiveness of

---

[20] Southern Negro Youth Congress papers, Moorland-Spingarn Research Center, Howard University. See also interviews with the Jacksons, 2002–present.

[21] *Ibid.*

[22] *Ibid.*

racial segregation. Jackson needed an audience like his wife when he voiced his purest frustration before he could more calmly generate the refined language he would share with a public audience.

With Cooper as his correspondent, Jackson could release his revulsion with segregation to a woman who was both a confidant and had the ability to address some of his concerns with action. After assuaging his disgust with his angry letter, Jackson sought to use his frustration productively by suggesting strategies for the SNYC to address the problems of segregation in the Army and in the South. Jackson discussed plans for veterans' issues in the postwar period. On April 15, 1944, Jackson suggested that the National Council of the SNYC establish a Veteran's Commission. The Commission, Jackson offered, "would have as its objective the formulation of plans and activities for the promotion of soldier welfare during the war [and] for the integration of Negroes in all post-war soldier welfare programs."[23] A veteran's commission was established, and Executive Assistant to the Director of Selective Service, Colonel Campbell C. Johnson spoke at the SNYC's 1944 Atlanta Conference on the reintegration of black veterans into U.S. society.[24] In this respect, Jackson's letters illustrate how his raw emotional outrage elicited strategic suggestions that influenced the SNYC and the South.

Esther Cooper's letters contain a similar combination of disdain for the South and energy toward changing it. The insults she described to her husband were more subtle in nature, and the way she expressed her frustration was somewhat more reserved. In one instance, Cooper wrote about a visit to a white doctor's office. Normally, Cooper visited black doctors, but Harriet needed to see a specialist, so Cooper's regular doctor recommended a white doctor he believed was progressive on race issues. Esther Cooper Jackson recalled that the doctor was so insulting that she was sick to her stomach.[25] Overall, though, Harriet's checkup went well "until the nurse called me Esther... and we had it!"[26] Addressing Cooper by her first name was clearly condescending and insulting on the part of the nurse. In addition, Harriet kept trying to run into the white waiting room to play with the other children. Cooper wrote:

> Ah! It's so senseless—sometimes I want to pack up and go to shield Harriet from the humiliations of being a Negro in the South. But perhaps she will be a wiser and more understanding person being here—we must live for a year in a country free from race prejudice for her sake.[27]

---

[23] JJ to EC, 15 April 1944, Jackson Papers.

[24] Colonet Campbell C. Johnson, Address delivered at the 6th Annual Conference of the Southern Negro Youth Congress, Atlanta, GA, 2 December 1944, Southern Negro Youth Congress Papers, Conferences, Moorland-Spingarn Research Center, Howard University.

[25] Esther Cooper Jackson conversation with Sara Rzeszutek, December 19, 2005, Brooklyn, NY.

[26] EC to JJ, 11 July 1945, Jackson Papers.

[27] *Ibid.*

The following day, however, Cooper attended a meeting for the Recy Taylor Committee, a class, and an Executive Board meeting for the SNYC.[28] In spite of—or perhaps in response to—the desire she expressed one day earlier to leave the South, Cooper fought steadfastly to end racial injustice, empower young black Southerners, and organize black leadership. This series of events that Cooper described in her letters indicates that segregation's offensiveness could function in two ways: it could drive blacks to leave the South, or, in Cooper and Jackson's case, it prompted activism and motivated leaders to work for greater justice. The exchanges between these two activists illustrate the ways in which black leaders planned activist strategies, anticipated their consequences, and hoped to change the world.

Given the atmosphere of the Ledo Road and his pride in his wife's activism, Jackson looked forward to working together with Cooper when he returned. Though he planned and hoped to work equally with his wife, he did express some dismay at her pace while he was absent. He wrote, "Your letters read like 'My Day' by Super Woman ... on reading your letter, I said to myself, 'It isn't necessary for anyone to be that busy, not even Stalin' ... Does this letter read like I'm sore? Well, I am ... I figured we'd have a busy time together 'changing the world' when I got back. But at the pace you're going all I'll have to do is live in it."[29] Jackson's frustration grew primarily out of concern about the negative consequences of Cooper's pace on her health, even though he suggested that he might be a bit jealous of the contribution Cooper made without him. He wrote, "Take it easy, Honey. There is just no sense in tearing yourself to pieces so early in the game. If you don't, I'll be spending my post war vacation nursing you, and all those rosy dreams we cherish will be still-born."[30]

Jackson was also concerned about Cooper's safety. Part of her busy schedule entailed visiting small towns in Alabama to investigate riots, rapes, and lynchings for the SNYC. For instance, Cooper visited Abbeville and Eufaula, Alabama to investigate two rape charges. She wrote, "The lynch spirit surrounds Eufaulia [sic]. All Negroes are ordered off the streets by 9 o'clock (We left at 8:30). The highway police & M.P.'s were called in by Gov. Sparks."[31] Jackson replied, "I don't like the idea of you taking trips into these little lynch towns on riot investigations ... one out of the family in enemy country at a time is enough, my sweet!"[32] Jackson's worries and frustrations, though, were ultimately tempered by the pride he took in his wife's success. The couple, in this instance, became an ideal representative of the Double

---

[28] EC to JJ, 12 July 1945, Jackson Papers. Recy Taylor was a black woman from Abbeville, Alabama who was gang-raped by a group of white men. The SNYC worked to attain justice on her behalf. See Danielle L. McGuire, "'It was like All of Us Had Been Raped': Sexual Violence, Community Mobilization, and the African American Freedom Struggle," *The Journal of American History*, December 2004, http://www.historycooperative.org/journals/jah/91.3mcguire.html (29 Apr. 2006).

[29] JJ to EC, 13 August 1945, Jackson Papers.

[30] *Ibid.*

[31] EC to JJ, 21 July 1945, Jackson Papers.

[32] JJ to EC, undated, *Ibid.*

Victory campaign black Americans initiated during the war: Jackson was fighting for democracy abroad, and Cooper was fighting on the home front.

Safety concerns and jealousy aside, Jackson was proud of Cooper and wanted to change the world with his wife when he returned from war. On July 6, 1945 Jackson replied to a June 23 *Baltimore Afro-American* article by Irene West entitled, "Females Halfway to Hell." West disparaged women's new position in industry during the war. Jackson compared West's position on women's wartime activities to fascists, who "have always advocated such a program of shackling women to the penury of the kitchen as part of their design for the super-exploitation, oppression, and ultimate enslavement of *all* mankind."

Jackson's gendered analysis of the struggle against fascism was inherently linked to his interpretation of the black freedom struggle in the South. He continued, arguing that West's concerns about women could easily be employed by southern "mobs" aiming to drive black women from their war-industry jobs "back to the 'white folks' kitchen and $3.00 a week." He closed by offering his perspective on women's liberation and leadership in the United States, stating, "The measure of our civilization's progress is to be seen in the extent to which women have achieved their liberation from the tyranny of male domination and the degree of equality attained in all fields of endeavor... May [Irene West] some day encounter Mary McLeod Bethune, Thelma Dale, Jeanetta Welch Brown, or my own wife, Esther Cooper."[33]

For Jackson, understanding the wartime world and planning for the postwar world meant recognizing that struggles around gender were integral to the fight for democracy. Highlighting female activists including his wife would contradict any claims to the contrary. His own marriage to Esther Cooper was inextricably linked to his outlook on national and international politics.

Cooper and Jackson believed that racial problems in the South were unique, and considered many ways they could work to change their home. The couple were getting older, and staying with the Youth Congress did not seem like a practical plan. Instead, Jackson offered that they might work for the National Association for the Advancement of Colored People (NAACP). He saw that the NAACP had the potential to be productive in the South if it were administered under the proper leadership, stating, "W[alter]. White has long looked enviously at the SNYC 'miracle workers'. He has no doubt longed for such organizational talent to breathe life into the Southern section."[34] Jackson suggested that he and Cooper try to get jobs as regional directors for the southern NAACP and build it into a left-wing-oriented mass movement. He wrote, "The [Communist Party] in the South, strong in Negro membership, a trade union movement conscious of its role of ally of the Negro people in their struggle for democratic rights, plus the [Southern Conference for Human Welfare]—all would contribute toward the rapid

---

[33] JJ to Editor of *Baltimore Afro-American*, 6 July 1945, *Ibid.*
[34] JJ to EC, 18 August 1945. File 43, p. 21, *Ibid.*

rearing of a Negro people's movement in the South out of the womb of the NAACP."[35]

The activist themes in Cooper and Jackson's letters illustrate the urgency of pragmatic black struggle in the South alongside the idealism of two black communists who ultimately struggled toward radically restructuring the U.S. social and political culture. Cooper and Jackson were situated directly in what historian Nikhil Pal Singh calls "the intersection of state-oriented liberalism inclined to ameliorative reform and a relatively autonomous black activism inclined to acts of rebellion."[36] The couple represented the fluidity of black nationalism and internationalism, radicalism and liberal reform, and patriotism and its limits in the context of World War II. The war also offered Cooper and Jackson a new framework for understanding the black freedom movement in the context of global politics.

By linking black oppression in the U.S., particularly in the Jim Crow South, to the oppression of colonized peoples across the globe, leaders like Cooper and Jackson offered an interpretation of global conflict that resonated deeply with black Americans in the United States. Black Americans might have participated in the war through either military service or war industry employment, they might have contributed to the war effort by purchasing war bonds and appropriately rationing their goods, and they might have wholeheartedly believed that they could share in the experience of saving democracy. Participation and support of the cause, however, did not mean that blacks failed to critique the contradictions of World War II and fight to lessen the gap between democratic rhetoric and the undemocratic reality in which they and millions of subjugated people across the world lived.[37]

As a highly educated intellectual, Jackson was unique among his fellow soldiers. The average soldier was, as the historian John Morton Blum suggests, "a reluctant hero, a folk hero... just ordinary American boys... friendly and enthusiastic and sensible... as normal as if nothing had happened."[38] Historian Gary Gerstle elaborates, arguing that soldiers' understanding of what they were fighting for was grounded in a sense of loyalty to their unit. While some nationalism, or a sense of common American identity, came into play for soldiers, they did not fight "for flag or country, for the Marine Corps or

---

[35] *Ibid.*

[36] Nikhil Pal Singh, *Black Is A Country: Race and the Unfinished Struggle for Democracy*, Cambridge, MA: Harvard University Press, 2004, 118.

[37] C.L.R. James, "Why Negroes Should Oppose the War," in James, George Breitman, Edgar Keemer, and others, *Fighting Racism in World War II* (New York: Monad Press, 1980); Walter White, *A Rising Wind*, Garden City (NY: Doubleday, Doran and Company, Inc., 1945); Brenda Gayle Plummer, *Rising Wind: Black Americans and U.S. Foreign Affairs, 1935–1960* (Chapel Hill: University of North Carolina Press, 1996); Barbara Dianne Savage, *Broadcasting Freedom: Radio, War, and the Politics of Race, 1938–1948* (Chapel Hill: University of North Carolina Press, 1999); Penny Von Eschen, *Race Against Empire: Black Americans and Anti-Colonialism* (Ithaca: Cornell University Press, 1997).

[38] John Morton Blum, *V was For Victory: Politics and American Culture in World War II* (New York: Harcourt Brace Jovanovich, 1976), 58–59.

glory, or any other abstraction. They fight for one another."[39] Jackson's fellow black soldiers, given this background, were probably even less likely to develop a sense of what the war was about than the average white soldier, shedding light on how the practice of segregation had systematically excluded black Americans from the very basic elements of the democracy for which they were fighting.

Once Jackson was overseas, his own level of exposure to the world outside of the United States changed and he began to think about the blatant similarities between British colonialism in South Asia and segregation in the U.S. South. He had read political articles and books in the past about the nature of imperialism, but seeing it firsthand changed the importance of the issue for him. He wrote in January 1945, "I have seen nothing in Alabama or Mississippi to equal the brutality of some of these Kiplingesque buccaneers."[40] Jackson observed that the behavior of U.S. soldiers toward the indigenous population differed significantly from that of the colonists. For the most part, American G.I.'s were respectful of their hosts. He told Cooper, "It is to the undying credit of our troops that such exhibitions have been the exception...rather than the rule—especially (and naturally) have the Negro troops conducted themselves well in their relations with our Indian hosts."[41] Jackson had seen how black soldiers, who were far from the sort of worldly intellectual he was could still understand the injustices of colonialism and respond to the situation sympathetically because of their own experiences with Jim Crow.

For Jackson, the war illustrated the connections between the problems of black southerners and international concerns. Jackson was a well-educated and shrewd student of international politics. His letters juxtaposed black soldiers' awareness of the world around them with the stark relationship between the circumstances in colonial India and the segregated South. Jackson elaborated on the implications of colonialism for Western Europe, arguing, "The people of the Far East have been stirred mightily by the winds of freedom emanating from this Great War of National Liberation." Colonialism's power would not "be contained within the framework of [antebellum] colonial possession."[42] Jackson believed firmly in the Allied cause in spite of the U.S.'s paradoxical relationship with a war for democracy and its own black citizens. Yet witnessing British colonialism in India solidified Jackson's belief that fascism was not unique to the Axis; that World War II was truly a war to end racism regardless of its national origin. In other words, fascism and racial tyranny were global phenomena that did not stop at Germany, Italy, Japan, and Spain. Jackson's experience and analysis fit squarely into the internationalist discourse among black leaders during World War II.

---

[39] Gary Gerstle, *American Crucible: Race and Nation in the Twentieth Century* (Princeton: Princeton University Press, 2001), 232.

[40] JJ to EC, 15 January 45, Jackson Papers.

[41] *Ibid.*

[42] Esther Cooper Jackson, *This Is My Husband: Fighter for his People, Political Refugee*, New York: National Committee to Defend Negro Leadership, 1953, 28.

FIG. 2. **Esther Cooper with Vidya Kanuga of the Indian Students Federation at the World Youth Congress, London, November 1945.**

While James Jackson's internationalism was not unique, Esther Cooper's international experience and internationalist thought alongside her husband's stand out. In the war years, Esther Cooper Jackson recalls, "We'd covered the world between us."[43] In 1945, SNYC leaders selected Esther Cooper to represent the organization at the October World Youth Conference in London. She spent a great deal of time in her letters discussing the sorts of issues she would promote at the conference, and her experience was shaped by the connections between the U.S. South and the colonized world. In preparation for the conference, she wrote a bulletin on "the colonial question" for SNYC members and councils. She drew from a wide range of sources, including her husband's experiences and W.E.B. Du Bois's 1945 *Color and Democracy*.[44] She spent much of her time at the conference, both in sessions and socially, with delegates from colonies.[45]

After the Conference, the Soviet Anti-Fascist Youth Committee offered Cooper an opportunity to join an all-female delegation from the newly founded World Federation of Democratic Youth (WFDY) on a tour of

[43] Esther Cooper Jackson interview with Sara Rzeszutek, 15 March 2006, Brooklyn, NY.

[44] EC to JJ, 13 July 45, Jackson Papers.

[45] Esther Cooper to Louis Burnham, Southern Negro Youth Congress Papers, Correspondence, Moorland-Spingarn Research Center, Howard University.

war-ravaged Europe. Fixing some of this devastation was something Cooper simply had to do. Not only would she truly understand the war's costs, she would also have an opportunity to help change things. When the delegation arrived in Stalingrad, Cooper and the other women moved into the basement of a lone building that had not been destroyed in the war. The women from different countries would share stories, sing, and discuss ideas while witnessing the worst consequences of wartime devastation. In Stalingrad, Cooper and the WFDY delegation worked as assistant bricklayers, helping to rebuild the city.

Some of the other American women, Esther Cooper Jackson recalls, "were a little startled that I had left a young child."[46] Many of the women Cooper was with would later sacrifice either their activist ambitions or desires for family. Cooper and Jackson's egalitarian relationship and the connections they saw between personal and political life allowed each partner to contribute more broadly to the Black Freedom Movement and the cause of democracy in World War II than couples whose roles were confined to traditional gender norms.

James Jackson excitedly anticipated his reunion with his wife. After a long discussion of Indian nationalism and Britain's policies in wartime India, he wrote, "Freedom is in the air, on the march everywhere. Freedom for me lies over there where you are—'Till locked again in your arms I will not know freedom from all the pangs of lonliness [sic] that inhabit the silent chambers of my being."[47] Through Cooper and Jackson's World War II letters, the daily struggles against racism and the accompanying emotional victories and defeats, the connections between the context of war, European imperialism, American segregation, and the personal dynamics of a family disrupted by global conflict coalesce. The couple's open correspondence sheds unfiltered light on the human frustrations of life in the Deep South and the piercing psychological impact of war. For Cooper and Jackson, wartime also contributed to the way in which they constructed their marriage and planned their future together, separated by thousands of miles. Total war meant that no sector of life was untouched by global conflict. James Jackson and Esther Cooper's correspondence reveals that freedom needed to be "on the march everywhere," from the battlefield to the home, for the sake of its own triumph in World War II.

---

[46] ECJ interview with Sara Rzeszutek, 15 March 2006, Brooklyn, NY.
[47] JJ to EC, 24 January 1945, Jackson Papers.

FREEDOMWAYS

MICHAEL NASH and DANIEL J. LEAB

(This essay draws on Jean Carey Bond's comments made at the Oct. 28, 2006 symposium on the Jacksons)

FREEDOMWAYS was one of the most influential African-American literary and political journals of the 1960s and 1970s. Its subtitle, "A Quarterly Review of the Negro Freedom Movement," summed up what the journal was about (as cultural semantics changed during the Second Reconstruction it dropped the word "Negro" from its subtitle in 1969). According to Esther Jackson the journal's name FREEDOMWAYS was adopted from a landmark sociological study *Blackways of Kent*, a pioneering effort by the distinguished African American scholar-activist Hylan Lewis, whose multi-part study was one of the first to make the connection between cultural and political change and argued that the meaning of a subculture needed to be changed before one could hope to change the racial order. For Jackson the insights of Lewis, who had been a high school classmate of James Jackson and who believed that "the reality is that race is everywhere in the American context," became the central idea for FREEDOMWAYS.[1]

As Michael Anderson has shown in an essay that appears in this volume, one of the main models for FREEDOMWAYS was *Freedom*, a monthly tabloid size newspaper founded in 1951 by Paul Robeson (the noted actor, singer, and activist), along with Louis Burnham (a brilliant thinker, writer, and key figure in the gathering civil rights movement of the later 1940s and early 1950s). That publication, well described as a "radical Left political publication with a strong interest in culture," died in 1955, a victim of the Cold War Red Scare. Burnham, who had moved on to the Left-oriented *National Guardian*, and a friend Edward E. Strong, who had been active in various Left-wing youth groups and at one time had served as the SNYC Executive Secretary, seeing

---

[1] Esther Jackson interview with Michael Nash, October 2, 2008, archived in the Oral History of the American Left, Tamiment Library, New York University; "Pursuing Fieldwork in African American Communities: Some Personal Reflections of Hylan Lewis," in Benjamin P. Bower, et al., eds., *Against the Odds: Scholars Who Challenged Racism in the Twentieth Century* (Amherst, MA: University of Massachusetts Press, 2002), 143.

what they thought was a change in the American political climate given court cases diminishing McCarthyism laid plans for a "progressive" Black literary and political quarterly.[2]

Before their dreams could be realized Burnham and Strong died, but before passing away in 1960 at the young age of 45, Burnham had recruited his friend Esther Jackson to the venture. A very fortuitous choice, for she served during FREEDOMWAYS twenty-five year life span as "the journal's organizational center and anchor" (to use historian James Smethurst's apt characterization). As managing editor of the journal from its inception until the last issue she shaped its intellectual direction and was the energy behind it. Over the years there was some pressure to add white members to the editorial board, but this was resisted since FREEDOMWAYS had been conceived as a voice for the African-American community. The members of the editorial board changed over the years, as did its emphases in response to the changing temper of the times, but she saw to it that FREEDOMWAYS always spoke with a clear and unmistakable voice.[3]

A "collective" was organized to launch FREEDOMWAYS. Shirley Graham Du Bois served as "general editor" until the late 1960s. Esther Jackson recalls that W.E.B. Du Bois, on the basis of his many years experience as editor of the NAACP's journal *Crisis*, advised that the publication should combine serious scholarship and careful analysis with a popular accessible style. He also stressed that the journal not be published until there were enough funds and copy on hand to ensure the first year of publication. That moment arrived in April 1961, and FREEDOMWAYS was launched at a reception for several hundred people at the Hotel Martinique in New York City. The editorial in the first issue clearly stated the magazine's purpose and goals:

> FREEDOMWAYS is born of a necessity for a vehicle of communication which will mirror developments in the diversified and many-sided struggles of the Negro people. It will provide a public forum for the review, examination, and debate of all problems confronting Negroes in the United States.[4]

The organization and publication of FREEDOMWAYS took place against a background of increased civil rights activity. In the mid-1950s there were the Montgomery, Alabama bus boycott, as well as similar actions in Florida and South Carolina, as well as elsewhere in Alabama. Dr. Martin Luther King, Jr., emerged as an extraordinary leader who could help to focus people's energies on race issues. *Brown vs. Board of Education of Topeka, Kansas*, and its aftermath

---

[2]James Smethurst,"SNYC, *Freedomways*, and the Influence of the Popular Front in the South on the Black Arts Movement," *reconstruction: studies in contemporary culture*, 8 (#1, 2008), 11. It is an interesting comment on the quality of some research in this area that in Wilson Record, *Race and Radicalism: The NAACP and the Communist Party in Conflict* (Ithaca, NY: Cornell University Press, 1964), 176, that Burnham is listed as "James Burnham" which would have been a surprise to that ideologue.

[3] Smethurst, 14; Jackson interview with Nash; see FREEDOMWAYS files in the James and Esther Jackson Papers, Box 8, Tamiment Library, New York University, especially the correspondence files with Shirley Graham Du Bois.

[4] Jackson interview with Nash; FREEDOMWAYS, Vol. 1 (April 1961), 5–6.

FIG. 1. **W.E.B. DuBois, with his wife, Shirley Graham DuBois (left) and Esther Cooper Jackson (right) at the Freedomways office, 1961.**

struck hard against school segregation. The Southern Christian Leadership Conference (SCLC) was established. And in February 1960 students from a Black institution, North Carolina A & T, refused to leave a Woolworth lunch counter when refused service, prompting a wave of lunch counter sit-ins where African-Americans had been denied service. And these actions in turn spurred the founding of the Student Non-Violent Co-ordinating Committee (SNCC).

As well, during this period, the Nation of Islam and other Black nationalist groups were in motion, promoting separation instead of integration. These groups were encouraged by the anti-colonialist and revolutionary movements that were gaining traction in Africa, Asia, Latin America, and the Caribbean. The latter region saw the revolutionary transformation of Cuba, under the dynamic leadership of Che Guevera and Fidel Castro. Everywhere in what had come to be known as the Third World, people of color were in revolt. The citizens of the "undeveloped countries" were in the forefront in the fight against economic and social discrimination.

This was the maelstrom of political, social, and economic forces and events against which FREEDOMWAYS arose—one might almost say, organically. As Ernest Kaiser—the respected librarian and hard-working bibliographer who oversaw the building up of the Schomburg Center for Research in Black Culture, and a longtime stalwart supporter of the journal, once wrote "FREEDOMWAYS was the African-American magazine that had to come." This publication was not, in the well-chosen words of Jean Carey Bond, a veteran FREEDOMWAYS editor "the offspring of niche marketers looking to tap consumer pocketbooks." During its 25 years of life, the publication was "inextricably connected to what Black people were creating and struggling to achieve on the ground."[5]

The original "collective" which produced the early issues of FREEDOMWAYS in addition to Shirley Graham Du Bois and Esther Jackson included Dorothy Burnham (Louis Burnham's widow and an activist in her own right), Margaret Burroughs (a Chicago-based artist and teacher), John Henrik Clarke (a professor, prolific historian, Pan Africanist, and Black nationalist), and Alpheus Hunton (a leading Pan Africanist, writer, and close associate of W.E.B. Du Bois). They were all greatly influenced by Du Bois, evident not only in his involvement in the creation of the journal. Thanks to him FREEDOMWAYS was planned not only to reflect and hopefully influence the rising tide of activism in the U.S. but also to be international in scope and internationalist in orientation. One of Du Bois's legacies, passed on to editors of the journal over the years was identification with Africa: for him all peoples of African descent shared a common heritage shaped by slavery and European colonization. Consequently FREEDOMWAYS took on as part of its mission the reporting to its American readers on events in Africa and Asia, and to its readers there about the American civil rights movement.[6]

Even though its emphases changed during the publication's lifetime as events influenced editorial policies, FREEDOMWAYS was always outspoken in its response to events. During and after the civil rights revolution FREEDOMWAYS was a political and cultural voice of the movement. Looking back on its record some years after the journal ceased publishing two scholars have accurately summed up its editorial approach as one that "amplified the voice of radicalism in the African-American community." The journal never lost its militancy, evident from the very first issues. In Fall 1961 FREEDOMWAYS argued that the NAACP must change with time or be destroyed. A few years later it editorialized that Lyndon Johnson's Great Society "was not a serious effort to end poverty, but a sham, an exercise to end street demonstrations while holding on to the Black vote." In 1967, commenting on the riots in Newark and Detroit FREEDOMWAYS declared,

---

[5] Kaiser quoted in Jean Carey Bond, "Roots of the Fight for Rights: Esther Jackson and *Freedomways* Magazine," and Bond, http://www.blackagendareport.com/005/005h_icb_roots_of_fight4rights.html

[6] See "W.E.B. Du Bois: The American Negro and the Darker World," in Esther Cooper Jackson and Constance Pohl, eds., *FREEDOMWAYS Reader* (Boulder, CO: Westview Press, 2000), 111–118. See also the W.E.B. Du Bois oral history memoir (1961) in the records of the Communist Party, USA, Tamiment Library, New York University, for a fascinating perspective on his hopes for the revived civil rights movement of the late 1940s and 1960 and the connections he saw between the American movement and the Pan-Africanist struggles.

"it's that time, America. Grant Negroes freedom and equality or invite catastrophe."[7]

As FREEDOMWAYS evolved after its debut in 1961, the journal—in addition to such hard-hitting editorializing—also presented a wide array of articles, poetry, short stories, book reviews, and art work by eclectic but predominantly African-American contributors. Although occasionally publishing a white or Latino, the editorial board remained solidly African-American during the publication's long existence. (Per one interview with James and Esther Jackson the all African-American policy was "adamantly" followed, even though causing "friction between FREEDOMWAYS and some white Leftists, especially the prominent Communist historian Herbert Aptheker"). The journal conducted an interesting and wide-ranging readers' forum. FREEDOMWAYS concentrated on setting forth new material and art work, but also published older material which fit in with its editorial policies and it was felt should be seen again, such as efforts by movement participants like Louis Burnham, W.E.B. Du Bois, and Paul Robeson.[8]

Esther Cooper Jackson in her introduction to a *Freedomways Reader* published in the year 2000, over a decade after the journal ceased publication, in reviewing its contents, summed up "the main subjects" covered while recording "the freedom struggle" to be "the Southern movement, international solidarity, the movement in the North, Black scholarship, and arts and activism." In gearing up to deal with these subjects FREEDOMWAYS early on described its central mission in an editorial "Culture and the Cause of Black Freedom." After proclaiming the "American Negro is on the threshold of a new cultural renaissance," the editorial noted barriers confront "the Negro cultural worker...prejudice and discrimination keep back all but a trickle of...[their] creative works from public exposure." The editors asserted that FREEDOMWAYS in dealing with these impediments would grapple with important questions: "Is there a distinctive character of Negro cultural expression? What is American Negro culture as distinct from or as related to American culture? What are the esthetic forms and values most appropriate to the social functions of the cultural expression of American Negroes' status and freedom struggles and aspirations?"[9]

A review of the contents of the journal over the years indicates that in connecting politics and culture it did not give itself over to any particular cultural attitude, but did embrace activism in its broadest form. Perhaps the perceptive Black novelist John Oliver Killens has summed up best the journal's

---

[7] Manning Marable and Leith Mullings, eds., *Let Nobody Turn Us Around: Voice of Resistance, Reform, and Renewal—An African American Anthology* (London, New York: Rowan & Littlefield Publishers, Inc., 2000), 374; FREEDOMWAYS, Vol. 6 (#1, 1966), 101, Vol. 7 (#2, 1967), 151.

[8] James and Esther Jackson interview, quoted in Smethurst, 15; Aptheker, however, as Ian Rocksborough-Smith points out, "remained on good enough terms" with FREEDOMWAYS "to attend the magazine's fundraisers...." (Rocksborough-Smith, "'Filling the gap': Intergenerational black radicalism and the Popular Front ideals of Freedomways magazine's early years, 1961–1965," *Afro-Americans in New York Life And History*, 31(#1, January 1, 2007), fn5.

[9] FREEDOMWAYS, Vol. 2 (#2, 1962), 117–118.

editorial ideology: "Black nationalist with a socialist perspective." In the process the older works of established Black writers such as Arne Bontemps, Gwendolyn Brooks, Sterling Brown, Langston Hughes, Killens, Claude McKay, and Margaret Walker were published (as were newer works when issued). Younger talents such as Nikki Giovanni, June Jordan, Audre Lorde, Paule Marshall, Clayton Riley, and Alice Walker were introduced to the reading public by FREEDOMWAYS. It provided a publishing venue for a generation of aspiring African-American authors struggling to find an outlet for their writing. The work of older visual artists such as Jacob Lawrence and Charles White was reproduced and commented on as was the output of practioners of the newer currents in Black art such as Romare Beardon, Elizabeth Catlett, Tom Feelings, and Cheryl Hanna. Some of the younger Black artists produced some memorable cover art for FREEDOMWAYS.[10]

Political commentary with wide-ranging and divergent views were exercised in FREEDOMWAYS by Angela Davis, Jesse Jackson, Martin Luther King Jr., and Whitney M. Young Jr. (at the time head of the Urban League). In addition to those already mentioned, among those who contributed to its pages were the entertainers Harry Belafonte, Ossie Davis, Ruby Dee, and Abbe Lincoln, the poets Pablo Neruda and Derek Walcott, the authors James Baldwin, Lorraine Hansberry, and Julian Mayfield, and in keeping with the strictures of W.E.B. Du Bois, important statesmen such as Cheddi Jagan (Guyana), Kwame Nkrumah (Ghana), and Julius Nyerere (Tanzania). A number of Black legal talents, including the late Haywood Burns (splendid head of the NAACP Legal Defense Fund), Derek Bell (a Harvard Law Professor and noted legal scholar), and Bruce Wright (an outspoken New York City judge), dealt with various aspects of jurisprudence of interest to African-Americans (such as affirmative action and the role of the courts in criminal justice).

Special issues were published on the diverse locations of the Black struggle including Harlem, Mississippi, the Caribbean, and Southern Africa; on population groups such as Mexican-Americans and Native Americans; on various individuals such as W.E.B. Du Bois, Lorraine Hansberry, Paul Robeson, and Charles White. FREEDOMWAYS's editors did not flinch from handling touchy topics. It was among the earliest opponents of the Vietnam War. In Spring 1965, Jack O'Dell (a former Party member and merchant marine radical, who after being Red-baited "vanished from the SCLC office" where he held a key fund-raising position "to join the staff of FREEDOMWAYS" as an Associate Editor, becoming a key voice on the editorial page) argued for American withdrawal from Vietnam. And shortly thereafter came "non-White" economist Robert Browne's "The Freedom Movement and the War in Vietnam," the first article critical of the war in a Black journal; a vigorous critic of America's Vietnam policy, Browne, who was

---

[10] John Oliver Killens, "Lorraine Hansberry: On Time." in Esther Cooper Jackson, *Freedomways Reader* (New York: Dodd, Mead, 1980), 337.

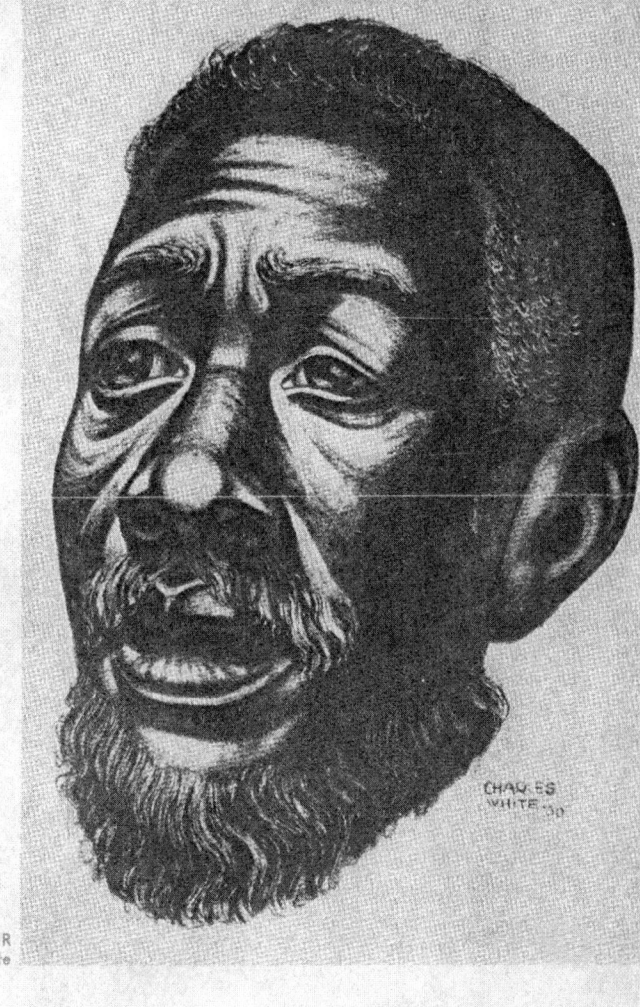

Freedomways

A QUARTERLY REVIEW OF THE NEGRO FREEDOM MOVEMENT

WILLIAM STYRON'S
DILEMMA

On *The Confessions
of Nat Turner*

Loyle Hairston

THE UNITED STATES
IN SOUTH AMERICA

Cheddi Jagan

THE SYSTEM OF
POLICE BRUTALITY

C. E. Wilson

THE AFRICAN ROOTS
OF WAR

W. E. B. Du Bois

Robert S. Browne reviews
Lomax's *Thailand*

Reviews of Other
Current Books

NAT TURNER
by Charles White

Vol. 8, No. 1 • Winter 1968 • (First Quarter) • $1.00

Fig. 2. *Freedomways,* **cover art by Charles White, Winter 1968.**

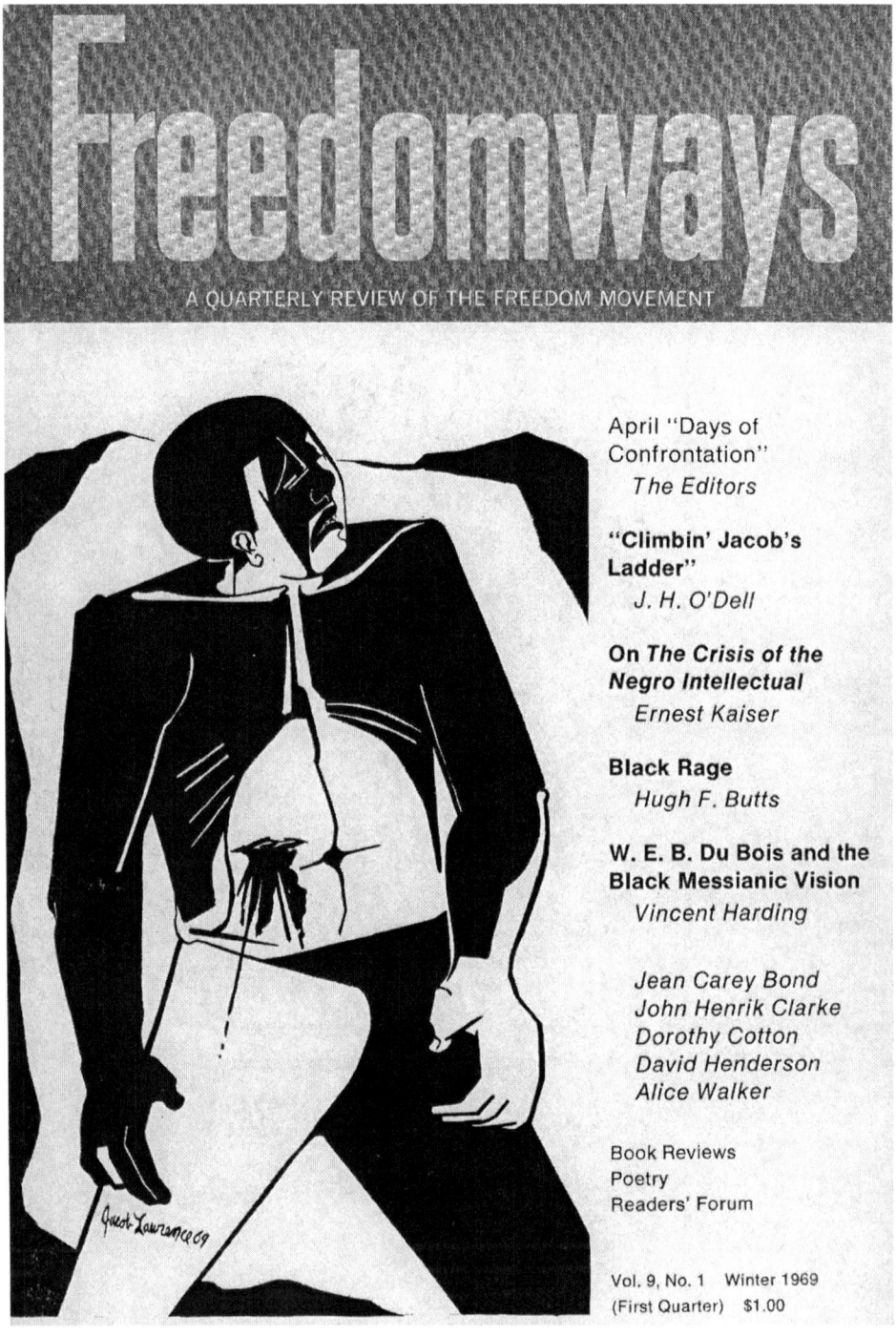

FIG. 3. *Freedomways*, cover art by Jacob Lawrence, Winter 1969.

"a veteran of economic development work in Cambodia and Vietnam," found it "discredited" and "racist."[11]

The editors were not always of one mind. There was vigorous discussion as the editors struggled to find a balance between domestic and international coverage. Shirley Graham Du Bois, who had joined her husband in self-exile in Ghana, wrote questioning the editors about their rationale for featuring mainstream writers such as James Baldwin. She also advocated more emphasis on the Pan-African movement, the situation in the Middle East, and the role of the Soviet Union. In 1964 as plans were laid for an issue honoring W.E.B. Du Bois she urged that Malcolm X be included and that an article by Kwame Nkrumah be published. This met with some resistance, as the editors thought FREEDOMWAYS should emphasize American developments and the struggle for integration rather than Black nationalism.[12]

In 1968 Esther Jackson insisted that NAACP chairman Roy Wilkins be allowed to contribute to a special issue honoring the late W.E.B. Du Bois even though he had not been treated well by the NAACP executive or the association during the McCarthy era, and relations had become strained. Shirley Graham Du Bois, who had joined her husband in his self-exile in Ghana strongly objected, but Jackson prevailed, saying the centennial celebration would be incomplete without some contribution from Wilkins and the NAACP—which Du Bois helped found and with which he had been associated with for many years. There were other controversies between Shirley Graham Du Bois and the editorial board, in part occasioned by her sojourn so far from New York City, and over time she became less involved with the publication.[13]

Shirley Graham Du Bois was one of the women who were present from the beginning. As Esther Cooper Jackson and Constance Pohl noted in their collection of FREEDOMWAYS writing, Black women were at the heart of the collective that established the publication. Other women involved included Augusta Strong, Jean Carey Bond, and Ruby Dee. Angela Davis, early in her career, became a contributing editor.[14]

As the women's movement gained momentum in the 1960s FREEDOMWAYS published important nonfiction works by women writers. Sarah Wright wrote what is still widely regarded as a seminal article about

---

[11] Taylor Branch, *Parting the Waters: America in the King Years, 1954–1963* (New York: Simon and Schuster, 1988), 851. (According to Rocksborough-Smith, O'Dell, who joined FREEDOMWAYS "largely due to his prior association with Esther and James Jackson through SNYC..." had a tremendous impact on the publication, "penning over sixty per cent of the staff editorials, writing twenty key strategy pieces over the twenty five years of the magazine's existence, and playing a central role in soliciting material from activists for publication"). Robert Browne, "The Freedom Movement and the War in Vietnam," FREEDOMWAYS, Vol. 5 (#4, 1965), 471; Wolfgang Saxon, "Robert S. Browne, 79, Dies; Economist and Advocate," *The New York Times*, August 15,2004, http://query.nytimes.com/gst/fullpage.html?res=9801EEDE123FF936A2575BC0A9629C8B63.

[12] John Henrik Clarke to Shirley Graham Du Bois, June 5, 1964, Jackson Papers, Box 9, Tamiment Library, New York University; Nash interview with Esther Jackson.

[13] Shirley Graham Du Bois to Esther Cooper Jackson, May 30, 1967, Jackson Papers Box 8, Tamiment Library, New York University; Nash interview with Esther Jackson.

[14] Jackson and Pohl, 205–207.

caricatures of women in contemporary literature (1965). Augusta Strong wrote tellingly about the role of Black women in the fight for freedom (1967). Angela Davis published an influential article on racism and rape in contemporary literature (1976). And Dorothy Burnham analyzed "False Theories about Women and Blacks" in an article on "Biology and Gender." As one would expect this commitment to women's literary voices created a certain amount of friction between the editorial board and contributing writers. Esther Jackson remembers that many male writers had difficulties working with women editors and resisted taking direction from them.[15]

FREEDOMWAYS ceased publication in 1985. After twenty-five years the editors were exhausted. The publishing world had also changed. African-American authors had many more and much better-paying outlets for their work than had been available a generation earlier. The journal, which always had operated on a shoe-string budget and was highly dependent on fund-raising to meet operational deficits, found it difficult to pay prevailing rates to authors. Advertising was minimal. FREEDOMWAYS, while not achieving the numbers attained by more mainstream left-wing publications such as *Nation*, had by 1968 a paid per issue circulation of over 5000, a significant increase from the first issues published in 1961. And a special issue such as the one memorializing W.E.B. Du Bois sold over 15,000 copies. But circulation stagnated.[16]

In an effort to make the publication as accessible as possible subscription rates were kept artificially low. Despite a quarter century of inflation, the cost of a subscription in 1985 to FREEDOMWAYS was only $7.50 a year. In 1961 the price had been $3.50. Even libraries that undoubtedly would have paid a great deal more (as they did for many periodicals) were charged the standard subscription rate. As a result, like many publications of its kind, FREEDOMWAYS did not have the financial resources to make the transition to the much more expensive world of computerized publishing in the 1980s.[17]

Ultimately, FREEDOMWAYS must been seen as more than a journal, thanks to the remarkable network which underlay its creation. During its life, especially in the early years FREEDOMWAYS was able to bring together a remarkable range of African-American intellectuals, artists, movement people, and political types, not only in its pages, but at the various events it organized. As James Smethurst admiringly pointed out FREEDOMWAYS's "sponsored events included book parties, readings, art shows, benefit concerts, holiday celebrations, tributes to important political and cultural figures" stretching across an array of "ideologies, age cohorts, and artistic...disciplines mixing 'high' and 'popular' culture...."[18]

While many other important and African-American publications were published during FREEDOMWAYS's twenty five years of existence, few lasted as long or had such an impact. In our opinion FREEDOMWAYS was in

---

[15] Nash interview with Esther Jackson.
[16] Nash interview with Esther Jackson; Rocksborough-Smith, 6.
[17] Nash interview with Jackson.
[18] Smethurst, 17.

many ways unique because of the outstanding breadth and depth of its coverage and its ability to serve as a respected, influential platform for the views of the diverse leading actors in the significant events that spanned the journal's life.

Moreover, as Ian Rocksborough-Smith has persuasively argued, FREEDOMWAYS provided a valuable link between the activists of the 1930s and 1940s, who survived McCarthyism, and "the civil rights movement and Black political discourse of the early and mid-1960s." These women and men brought with them "their experiences in Popular Front anti-racist organizations such as the Council on African Affairs, the National Negro Congress, and the Civil Rights Congress." FREEDOMWAYS therefore served as an important "intergenerational" link that connected organizations such as the SNYC and other Popular Front Black groups with SNCC and SCLC.[19]

Much of the quarterly's justified renown is due to the values, drive, and thought of Esther Cooper Jackson, an extraordinary person and an exemplary leader. Since an early age she lived her life conspicuously and with clarity of purpose and mind. It has been said about W.E.B. Du Bois that he saved every piece of his correspondence from the age of twelve. As the saying goes "even then he knew" that he would work hard to construct a life of purpose and consequence. Esther Cooper Jackson is that kind of person, and FREEDOMWAYS is but one of the many projects which benefited from her life and work.

---

[19] Rocksborough-Smith, 1–20, passim.

James and Esther Jackson: A Personal Perspective

MAURICE JACKSON

I've always had a love for history. My appreciation of history deepened and broadened during my college years and then after graduation in the course of participating in many movements and struggles. Of course, back in those days black youth for the most part had to discover African American history on their own. It wasn't offered in the curricula of most public schools or public or private universities in those days. My personal search to try to understand the present through an appreciation of the past was a veritable treasure hunt. Going to used book stores, perusing the dusty stacks of libraries, attending lectures, and taking counsel with community elders.

As my people and our country elevated themselves with civil rights triumphs, and as our nation suffered tortuous divisions, devastating defeats, and the incalculable loss of life in Vietnam, I often found myself wondering: Why is it that we reject history's lessons? Why are we so arrogant as to believe that the past can teach us nothing? How has it come about that we frequently elect leaders who pursue policies that mock history's warnings in a manner that prove the correctness of Karl Marx's rejoinder to Hegel's contention that history repeats itself: "He forgot to add," Marx commented, "first as tragedy, second as farce." Something to think about as we witness things going from bad to worse to terrible to horrific in Iraq.

Of course, unlike George W. Bush, I had had the distinct privilege for more than half of my adult life of knowing history up close and personal. Contrary to the President, who has enjoyed a lifetime of advantage and unaccountability, I have had the extraordinary advantage of being able to take counsel from living history which helped me to learn to hold myself accountable to history. As the late Ann Richards said of the President's father George Herbert Walker Bush and could of him "poor George, he does not know any better—he was born with a silver foot in his mouth." But there has been no silver lining or no "crystal stairs" in the words of Langston Hughes for the American people under King George the Second's rule.

The President may come from a family with a fortune, but starting thirty some years ago it's been my great fortune to have been nurtured by a family of living, loving, making, breaking, walking, talking history—Dr. James E. Jackson and Esther Cooper Jackson. Esther and Jack if they lived in their home state of VA would be known as a FFV. This is the name given to African Americans in Virginia families of distinction as a way to counter the white image.

Jim and Esther together and each in his and her own right are like the great jazz masters who look back from their senior years and proudly say "I have spent my entire life doing what I love to do—create good music." Jim and Esther are able to look back and say with pride and a personal sense of satisfaction, "We devoted ourselves to each other, to our daughters, and to the great causes of our times."

As a young couple they ventured to Birmingham, Alabama in the 1930s to help establish the Southern Negro Youth Congress. It was then that they developed life-long friendship and fellowship with W.E.B. Du Bois and Paul Robeson. Under the tutelage of Ralph Bunche, Jim worked on the Gunnar Myrdal project. Esther, as a graduate student did a pioneering study of Black female domestic workers. Jim fought on the Burma Road during World War II.

But let me shift to the personal and political if I may. Some thirty years ago I first met Jack at the Ambassador Hotel in DC. That is the same place that Langston Hughes worked at years before – maybe the inspiration for his "BUSBOYS AND POETS." Jack was teaching at Antioch College along with Jack O'Dell and Hosea Hudson and so I got wonderful educations. Eventually, Jack started staying at my little apartment—with no food but stocked with Ice Cream when he came to town—of course Esther did not know. And when I got married and moved and had kids—Jack always moved with us. In the early 70's I also began to stay with him and Esther, first in the small room that was Jack's office and in later years when it was overrun in the living room—I will get back to that.

From then on they were like parents to me. Now mind you I never really lived in a place with a man and woman, a father and a mother—I first lived with my divorced mother—then with Daddy Bert and Ma Vie when I was 3 or 4. He worked on the railroad and she was a cafeteria worker. But my mother not wanting to separate me and my older brother sent us to the Piney Woods of Alabama where she was born, to live with my wonderful grandmother, a simple washerwoman. She refused to work in the houses of the rich and not so rich white folks, as most African American women did, and preferred to "take in wash" or wash clothes. While I am deeply spiritual, I am not a religious man, but if it is so that God made man and women in his own image then the mold was cast with Pearl Lee Dickinson.

When I go to the prisons to teach I carry a book edited by Herb Boyd, BROTHERMAN. It is a collection of the works of "Strong Black Men" in the words of Jack's old friend Sterling Brown. And we read Frederick Douglass and W.E.B. Du Bois, and Paul Robeson and James Jackson. (And we also read

The Freedomways Reader edited by Esther Cooper Jackson). Sometimes the prisoners decry the fact that they grew up in a household and the father may not have been there or had to work all the time. I just tell them that my grandmother raised me and that she was "more of a man than any man that I have ever known." And I do not mean in a manly sense but in the sense of inner strength—of humanity, decency.

But in fact I never really knew what I had missed until I saw Esther and Jack interact on a daily basis. And what great lesson I learned about commitment and devotion. I experienced the gentle yet firm prodding of Esther to write every phrase correctly and to check every point. I suppose in one way I went back to school to study 18th century history because I knew that if I wrote about the SNYC days—I would have to be almost perfect—and meet Esther's high expectations.

At any rate they have played such a great part in my own development. The nightly discussions for many years when I would come to NYC sometimes every other week and most times every other month or so. But there are 3 small events I want to share.

First are the great adventures with Jack. The most notable was at a Conference of Black officials in Richmond, VA, Jack's home town. One of the high points was to watch Jack and his old buddy then Detroit Mayor Coleman Young interact about the old days in Birmingham and Detroit. While there he took me and Jim Steele on a drive in Richmond—Jack had driven down. And he took me to Douglass Court and Jackson Ward—maybe I have them backwards—but at any rate Jack points there—and the car goes the other way and he then points here and the car careens the other way. Well, we were glad to get out of Richmond. But then as I recalled the story to Esther—she told me that as soon as Jack got out from the underground the first thing he did was to pack HIS LADIES in a car and they headed out west to Mexico and the Grand Canyon.

Then there were the times when Jack and I would leave his and Esther's apartment in Brooklyn to go to a meeting at Party Headquarters on 23 Street in Chelsea. Well Jack never left without forgetting something and Esther always would count to 10 and wait at the door with something in her hand—one time it was his Russian hat—you know the Brezhnev one—the big fur—and I also had one—but mine more like the type Ahmad Karazai the Afghan leader wears.

Well, we get his hat and go to the subway and all of a sudden this 4′2″ or so kid swoops to Jack's head and swished his hat off of his head—Jack was initially startled and outraged—and cussed like a Boy Scout—and me—a man who had worked on ships knew some crusty language—well in those days I was a marathon runner and could have caught the lad except that I caught cramps—not runners cramps mind you—but stomach cramps—as I was bowled over in laughter—it was and is one of the funniest moments that I remember. Well when we got home—the first thing that Esther asked James Jackson about was that hat—it is cold outside and I know you took that hat. She was so serious and of course I left it to Jack to tell her the story.

And lastly there were the many nights we would talk until the wee hours. Now it was not until some years back that I stopped any alcohol consumption that I realized what a sweet tooth was—and why Jack so loved his ice cream. Many a night especially in the living room we would talk and Esther would insist on helping me make the bed—and inevitably Jack would fall asleep in MY BED—and you could just imagine trying to get him up as he declares that he was not sleeping and continued to tell whatever story that he told.

These are just a few of my great memories of Esther and Jack. I am invited to dinner with the outgoing UN Secretary General, Kofi Annan at Georgetown University where I am a Professor in the History Department. Not bad for a kid from the projects. I remind the Secretary General of the NYU event and of the role that Jack played in aiding Dr. Du Bois to go to Ghana to work on his, "Encyclopedia Africana." There is nothing that could compare with my sense of joy in being at the NYU event and my great love and gratitude to Esther and Jack.

"Death for Negro lynching!" The Communist Party, USA's Position on the African American Question

TIMOTHY JOHNSON

"Men make their own history, but they do not make it as they please; they do not make it under self-selected circumstances, but under circumstances existing already, given and transmitted from the past."
    Karl Marx, *The Eighteenth Brumaire of Louis Bonaparte.*

James and Esther Jackson, along with their colleagues, Edward Strong, Louis Burnham, and others too many to mention, made history. Through their work in the Southern Negro Youth Congress they challenged racial segregation in the U.S. South during the 1930s and 1940s. They organized tobacco workers, agitated for the right of African Americans to vote, and demonstrated against lynching. Yet, in spite of their individual heroism, they did not make history "under self-selected circumstances." The context of their actions was their membership or association with the Communist Party of the United States of America (CPUSA). In the late 1920s and early 1930s the CPUSA highlighted the struggle of African Americans for liberation and equality as an inseparable part of the struggle of the working class. In so doing they broke new ground for left-wing organizations in the United States and created a template that nearly all socialists and left-wing organizations have since followed. How was that template created, what were some of the immediate results which followed?

The political roots of the CPUSA lay within the social democratic movement. The social democratic position on the African American question is often characterized by a quote from Eugene V. Debs in an article written in the *International Socialist Review*. Debs wrote, "We have nothing special to offer the Negro, and we cannot make separate appeals to all the races."[1]

Although this statement could be interpreted as rather dismissive, Debs was actually sympathetic to the plight of African Americans, as his more complete statements demonstrate. In the same article Debs added that, "...so thoroughly is the south permeated with the malign spirit of race hatred that even socialists are to be found, and by no means rarely, who either share

---

[1] Debs, Eugene V., "The Negro and the Class Struggle," *The International Socialist Review*, (#5, 1903), 260.

Fig. 1. Louis Burnham addressing longshoremen and teamsters at a right to vote rally, New Orleans, 1943.

directly in the race hostility against the negro, or avoid the issue, or apologize for the social obliteration of the color line in the class struggle."[2] Debs' position was that race hatred was a direct attribute of economic inequality created by the capitalist system and would disappear through the process of the class struggle and the eventual triumph of socialism. He argued that since the issue of social inequality was a mere mask of the root problem of economic inequality, all social agitation on this issue was pointless, concluding there was "no negro question outside of the labor question—the working class struggle."[3] While Debs repeatedly expressed his sympathy for the victims of racism and understood its historic roots, he firmly believed that any separate agitation on racism was simply a diversion from the class struggle.

Debs' position was a centrist one within the Socialist Party (SP) at the turn of the twentieth century. Although the issues of racism and African American oppression were rarely openly debated within the SP there were a number of Party activists who took public positions on these issues. At one end of the spectrum were white socialists such as Mary White Ovington, a founder of the

[2] Debs, 257.
[3] Debs, 259.

NAACP, and a number of African American activists. At the other end were SP leaders such as Victor Berger, who were outright racists.[4] In a 1913 article in the *New Review*, Ovington regretfully acknowledged that the only two organizations that had expressed an honest concern for the plight of African Americans were the NAACP and the Industrial Workers of the World (IWW). She added, "I wish I might cite the Socialist party, the party I so love," but lamented that some of the southern sections were as racist as the Democratic Party. She recognized the solitary resolution on the African American question that was passed at the Socialist Party convention in 1901, but added, "...there has been no word since."[5] The renowned African American scholar W.E.B. Du Bois, briefly a member of the Socialist Party, also took it to task for its dismissal of racism and African American oppression. "No recent convention of Socialists," he wrote in 1919, "has dared to face fairly the Negro problem."[6] Berger, a Socialist party leader from Wisconsin, was described by historian Sally Miller thusly, "as a unionist he saw the Negro as unorganizable, as a socialist he thought him irrelevant, and as a German he believed the Negro, and indeed all others, to be inferior."[7]

The position of the rank and file and local leaders, which may be a more accurate assessment of the tenor of the organization, can be partly assessed through the few discussions on this issue at the Socialist Party conventions. The most sustained discussion on the African American question occurred at the Socialist Party unity convention in Indianapolis in 1901, which marked the merger of the Social Democratic Party and the Socialist Labor Party of America. At that convention a special committee drafted a resolution on the African American question (the resolution to which Ovington referred). The African American members who drafted the resolution noted that they needed a clear statement to assist in their organizing efforts in the African American community. The original draft recognized the "peculiar" position of African Americans as a result of chattel slavery and racial discrimination at the workplace, offered the "heartiest sympathy" of the socialists, and called upon African Americans to join the Socialist Party. However, the fourth clause of the resolution, which contained a condemnation of lynching, proved to be the most controversial. It stated:

> Whereas, this position of the Negro has resulted in industrial war being declared against him, this resulting in the persecution of innocent members of

---

[4] Sally M. Miller, "The Socialist Party and the Negro, 1901–20." *The Journal of Negro History*. 36 (1971), 220–229.

[5] Mary White Ovington. "The Status of the Negro in the United States." *The New Review*. September 1913, 748.

[6] W.E.B. Du Bois, "Socialism and the Negro Problem," *The New Review*, January 1913, 138. In addition to Du Bois there were a number of other African American intellectual/activists involved with the Socialist party at various times. One of the more prominent was Hubert Harrison. See Jeffery Perry's *A Hubert Harrison Reader* (Middletown, CT: Wesleyan University Press, 2001) and Hubert Henry Harrison, "The Father of Harlem Radicalism". The Early Years: 1883 through the founding of the Liberty League and the "Voice" in 1917 (unpublished Ph.D. diss., Columbia University, 1986).

[7] Miller, 222.

the race, their severe punishment for trivial offenses, their lynching, burning and disenfranchisement, contrary to the moral law that all civilized people are supposed to obey, and contrary to the constitutional law of the land . . .[8]

As the discussion of the resolution unfolded, most objections were centered on the difficulties that taking such a strong position against racism would create in attempting to organize white workers. Delegate Simons questioned the veracity of the statement about innocent people being lynched and further argued that if the resolution emanated from the convention,

> . . . we are going to force the comrades of the south to debate not the question of the relation of socialism to the Negro, but the relation of a whole lot of social questions to the Negro . . . In other words we are going to force them to debate what we do not want to, that is, debate the race question.[9]

Delegate Costley, an African American and one of the composers of the resolution, insisted that his presentation of the resolution was offered as a socialist, not an African American. He added, "This is presented as a matter of tactics. It will enable the negro organizer to go among the negroes." Directing his comments to Simon, Costley noted, "There is not a word in that resolution that is not absolutely based on fact . . . We don't want that document as anything more than a lever to work among the negroes of the United States."[10] Several delegates argued that the Socialist Party needed to adopt a principled position on African Americans irrespective of the difficulties that might ensue in attempting to attract white workers to the Party. Delegate Hayes noted that, "I as a socialist do not propose to follow the footsteps of the hypocritical Democratic and Republican parties that are always straddling questions." He added,

> . . . the proper thing to do is to adopt it as presented by our comrade so that he can go out among his people and get a hearing to present these questions to them. I believe this will be the means or the beginning of making an inroad upon the class of people that we have been unable to reach . . .[11]

Delegate Spring, while adding that he bore no racial prejudice and sympathized with the need for socialist propaganda aimed at African Americans, reminded the delegates that "this document is not going to be confined solely to the Negro population." Spring argued that publicizing the document would lead to problems among southern whites and concluded ". . . when this convention takes the matter up they should take it up so as to follow the line of least resistance between the colored and the white laborers of this country." Delegate Herron retorted, "Without any regard to what we want or do not want, the race question is a fact." He added, ". . . it would be better

---

[8] Socialist Party of America, Papers, 1897–1963. Series I, Part D, National Convention Proceedings. July 30, 1901. (Glen Rock, NJ: Microfilming Corporation of America, 1975), 20.

[9] *Ibid.*, 22.

[10] *Ibid.*, 24.

[11] *Ibid.*, 25.

for the socialist movement to lose the votes and the support of the white men in the South than to evade this race question."[12]

Ultimately the resolution was amended to drop the reference to lynching and was passed by the Indianapolis convention. Two years after the convention Debs wrote, "...permit me to express the hope that the next convention may repeal the resolution on the negro question. The negro does not need them and they serve to increase rather than diminish the necessity for explanation."[13] As Miller summarized the Socialist party position on African Americans:

> The American Negro for the Socialist party was, as aptly described by Ralph Ellison, "the invisible man." The party did not reject Negro membership—it stood for Negro suffrage when the issue arose—yet with the exception of a vocal minority, it doubted Negro equality and undertook no meaningful struggles against second-class citizenship.[14]

The Socialist Party seemed incapable of adequately grappling with the issue of African American oppression. Their ideology of class struggle politics did not make them immune from the racism that afflicted the country at large. The African American membership was too small to wage an effective fight to push for an appropriate position and, finally, there was no countervailing pressure from any other source that could force the party to commit itself to a program that recognized the special oppression of the African American people. These circumstances would change with the victory of the Bolshevik Party in the Russian Revolution, the founding of the CPUSA, and with the founding and organization of the Communist International."

The victory of the Bolshevik Party in the Russian Revolution of 1917 had a dramatic impact on socialist parties across the world. Most parties split, with the left-wing allying themselves to the new Soviet government and the Communist Party of the Soviet Union. Left-wing socialists in the United States were divided into two parties (the Communist Labor Party and the Communist Party of America) and endured a long faction-driven process overseen by the newly formed Communist International to unite into one party.

The composition of the Russian Empire, characterized by Bolshevik leader V.I. Lenin as a "prison of nations," had long presented Russian socialists with the task of creating a political program to incorporate the experience and demands of oppressed nations and nationalities into the socialist revolution. In addition, the Comintern operatives included a large number of revolutionaries from colonial countries. Given these two facts, along with the Comintern's vision of fashioning itself as the headquarters of world revolution, it was only natural that the Comintern would turn its attention to the question of the oppression of African Americans.[15]

---

[12] *Ibid.*, 26

[13] Debs, 260.

[14] Miller, 221.

[15] Much of the literature claims the push for a change in the CPUSA's line came from the Soviets. While the Soviet Communist Party undoubtedly held ideological sway within the Comintern, there were a number of other Communists who agitated for a clearer line on the African American question. Among

The Bolshevik position on the national question, the issue of oppressed nations and nationalities, was outlined in numerous works by Joseph Stalin, himself a member of the oppressed Georgian nation, and Lenin.[16] Under the Bolshevik position, oppressed nations and nationalities were viewed as critical allies in the working-class struggle. Communists were duty bound to support the right of oppressed nations to determine their own collective destiny (the right of self-determination) and to the rights of national minorities to be accorded formal equality under law. Under the leadership of the Comintern, communists from across the world gathered to discuss the African American question and sought to devise a program that was consistent with revolutionary Marxism. Ultimately their discussions led them to the view that African Americans were best categorized as an oppressed nation who were deserving of the right to self-determination. This oppressed nation, the Comintern reasoned, was located in the Black Belt area of the South, where African Americans composed a majority of the population.

The importance of placing Africans Americans within the categories of an oppressed nation and nationality was that they were no longer viewed as a "race" (with its implied hierarchies) distinguished from other minorities only by the severity of their oppression. Instead they were looked at as critical allies in the working-class struggle. Thus, viewing them as an oppressed nationality heightened the importance of political work by communists in the African American community. Unlike the Socialist Party, which largely viewed the "negro problem" through the prism of organizing white workers, communists were to make the struggle against national oppression an uncompromising plank in their program. Rather than viewing the struggle for African American rights as a hindrance to the struggle of organizing the broader working class, the communists recognized that there would never be an effective class struggle if it did not wage a fight against racism and national oppression. Lenin himself stated that "Nothing so much holds up the development and strengthening of proletarian class solidarity as national injustice."[17] Consequently, the struggle against national oppression was seen as indispensable in the struggle for proletarian revolution.

The African American question was discussed at a number of Comintern congresses. At the Second Congress (1920) U.S. Party leader John Reed

---

(footnote continued)

them was Harry Haywood, an African American former member of the African Blood Brotherhood who was in Moscow as a student, and two foreign Communists with experience derived from living in the United States. See Harry Haywood's Black Bolshevik: Autobiography of an Afro-American Communists, (Chicago: Liberator Press, 1978); V.B.Karnik's M.N. Roy: political biography, (Bombay: Nav Jagriti Samaj, 1978); Hyman Kublin's Asian Revolutionary; The Life of Sen Katayairta, (Princeton: Princeton University Press, 1964).

[16] Joseph Stalin, Marxism and the National Question: selected writings and speeches. (NY: International Publishers, 1941) and V.I. Lenin, "Critical Remarks on the National Question," Collected Works. (Moscow: Progress Publishers, 1972), Vol. 21, 17–51.

[17] Lenin, Collected Works, Vol. 21, 273.

spoke about the African American situation. He described the extreme oppression and exploitation of African Americans in the South and the North, but denied that national consciousness was a critical factor. He argued that:

> The Negroes do not pose the demand of national independence. A movement that aims for a separate national existence, like for instance the 'back to Africa' movement that could be observed a few years ago, is never successful among the Negroes. They hold themselves above all to be Americans, they feel at home in the United States. That simplifies the tasks of the communists considerably. The only correct policy for the American Communists towards the Negroes is to regard them above all as workers.[18]

Although Reed, representing the U.S. Communist Party, still saw the African American question as only an aspect of the broader class question, his comments did reveal that the communists had taken major steps forward from the position of the Socialist Party. His condemnation of racism, approving comments of the work of A. Philip Randolph and *The Messenger* magazine, and appeal for white workers to reject racism signified that the communists were prepared to take a new approach to African Americans. At the Third Congress (1921) the South African Communist Party suggested that the African American question be put on the next agenda.

At the Fourth Congress (1922) the decision was made to apply the "Theses on the National and Colonial Question" to the African American situation and a statement was issued that categorized the African American question as "an important part in the liberation struggle of the entire African race, and a "vital question of the world revolution."[19] Lenin's "Theses on the National and Colonial Question," submitted to the Comintern and slightly amended by the Indian communist M.N. Roy, was an attempt to provide the international communist movement with an orientation to the struggle of oppressed nations and nationalities.

At the Sixth and Seventh Congresses (1928 and 1930) the Comintern issued two major statements on the African American question. Both statements were framed by the "Theses on the National and Colonial Question," which were submitted to the Comintern by Lenin in 1920. The second of Lenin's theses statements read, "The Communist Party, as the avowed champion of the proletarian struggle to overthrow the bourgeois yoke, must base its policy, in the national question too, not on abstract and formal principles but, first, on a precise appraisal of the specific historical situation..."[20] In his preface to the theses Lenin requested additional information from Comintern delegates with information about specific national questions, included the question of "negroes in America." With Lenin's theses as a framework the Comintern

---

[18] Philip Foner and James Allen, eds., *American Communism and Black Americans: A Documentary History, 1919–1929* (Philadelphia: Temple University Press, 1987), 6.

[19] Jane Degras, ed, *The Communist International, 1919–1943, Documents*. Vol. III (N.Y.: Oxford University Press, 1965), 399–401.

[20] Lenin, *Collected Works*, Vol. 31, 145.

attempted to concretize a communist position on African American oppression and exploitation.[21]

The 1928 Comintern thesis reiterated the finding that African Americans constituted an oppressed nation and that self-determination was the correct demand for the Black Belt South. It stated,

> While continuing and intensifying the struggle under the slogan of full social and political equality for Negroes, which must remain the central slogan of our Party for work among the masses, the Party must come out openly and unreservedly for the right of Negroes to national self-determination in the southern states, where the Negroes form a majority of the population[22]

Shortly after the Sixth Congress, *The Communist*, the theoretical journal of the CPUSA, published its first major article on the African American question. Written by John Pepper, this article attempted to specify the Comintern directives on African American work by placing work among African Americans at the center of Party work. "The Communist Party," Pepper wrote, "cannot be a real Bolshevik Party without being also the Party of the liberation of the Negro race from all white oppression."[23] The article analyzed the class structure of the African American community, looking at the role of the working class, farmers, and the petit-bourgeoisie and highlighted the importance of the struggle against racism within the Communist Party. On the issue of self-determination, Pepper wrote

> The Workers (Communist) Party of America puts forward correctly as its central slogan: *Abolition of the whole system of race discrimination. Full racial, social, and political equality for the Negro people.* But it is necessary to supplement the struggle for the full racial, social and political equality of the Negroes with a struggle for their right of national self-determination. Self-determination means the right to establish their own state, to erect their own government, if they choose to do so.[24]

Pepper even went further than the Comintern and asserted that "The Negro Communists should emphasize in their propaganda *the establishment of a Negro Soviet Republic.*"[25] At the Seventh Congress, the Comintern issued a more detailed analysis of the African American question. It criticized the Party's

---

[21] Although Lenin wrote no detailed study of African Americans, he had noted in one essay that, "In the United States, the Negroes...account for only 11.1 per cent. They should be classed as an oppressed nation, for the equality won in the Civil War of 1861–65 and guaranteed by the Constitution of the republic was in many respects increasingly curtailed in the chief Negro areas." He went on to draw a distinction between African Americans and European immigrants, noting that Europeans were being rapidly assimilated into the American nation. Lenin, *Collected Works*, Vol. 23, 245.

[22] Degras, 399–401.

[23] John Pepper, "American Negro Problems," *The Communist*, Oct. 1928, pp. 628–638. Pepper was a pseudonym for Joseph Pogany, a Hungarian communist and Comintern operative who was sent to work with the CPUSA in the early 1920's. He engaged in the debate on the African American question at the Sixth Congress and this article is presumed to be the substance of his presentation. See Foner and Allen, p. 178 and Bryan D. Palmer's *James P. Cannon and the Origins of the American Revolutionary Left, 1890–1928* (Urbana: University of Illinois Press, 2007), 188–195.

[24] Pepper, 629.

[25] Pepper, 632.

understanding and implementation of the Sixth Congress position. Specifically it accused the CPUSA of an "underestimation" of the African American question and an overall "lack of clarity" on the right to self-determination.[26]

The Seventh Congress thesis sought to reemphasize the concept that the African American question was of a special type due to the peculiar history of the United States, including chattel slavery and legal segregation. "This whole system of 'segregation' and 'Jim-Crowism'," the statement continued, "is a special form of national and social oppression under which the American Negroes...suffer." It argued for communists to struggle for all democratic rights for African Americans and (interestingly, in light of the Socialist Party's vacillation on the issue of lynching) added that "One of the first Communist slogans is: Death for Negro lynching!" It placed the struggle for equal rights for African Americans as "one of the most important parts of the proletarian class struggle in the United States"—adding that it was also the responsibility of white workers to be in the leadership of this struggle. And, in a concept well ahead of its time for a multi-racial organization, it supported the right of African Americans to engage in armed self-defense against the terrorism of racist organizations such as the Ku Klux Klan.[27]

Finally, it attempted to clarify the slogan of the right to self-determination. The Comintern noted that self-determination was one of three demands in the Black Belt. The other demands were for the redistribution of land by confiscating it from plantation owners and turning it over to landless sharecroppers and the establishment of a unified political system within the Black Belt, where African Americans constituted a majority of the population. However, it was the demand for the redistribution of land that would make possible the other demands. It argued "Without this revolutionary measure, without the agrarian revolution, the right of self-determination of the Negro population would be only a Utopia or, at best, would remain only on paper without changing in any way the actual enslavement."[28]

For the next several years, *The Communist*, the CPUSA's theoretical journal, followed the Comintern decision with a series of articles addressing various aspects of the political line on the African American question. These articles represented the most significant attention the Communist Party had given to this issue. The thrust of the articles were aimed at correcting mistaken notions about the new policy, arguing against misinterpretations of the policy, and raising the importance of the struggle against white racism (chauvinism) within the party. Joseph Prokopec contributed an article that sought to demonstrate that African Americans were not a race, but a national minority. Alternately quoting from the Comintern thesis and enunciating party policy, he drew distinctions between a "race" and

---

[26]"Resolution on the Negro Question in the United States," *Political Affairs*, 10 (#2, 1931), 153–167.

[27] The African Blood Brotherhood, composed of African American's and Caribbean Americans (many who later joined the Communist Party) had called for armed self-defense years before, but this may be the first time a non-Black organization issued such a call.

[28]"Resolution on the Negro Question in the United States," *Political Affairs*, 160.

a "nationality," arguing that to "view African Americans as simply a racial group was to accept bourgeois theories of race and ignore the social and economic consequences of national oppression."[29] While attempting to clarify the right to self-determination he noted, "just as in the case of any national revolutionary movement, so in the case of Negroes in America, the slogan for the right of self-determination cannot be an isolated slogan of struggle." He added that programs supported by the party "should include not only the economic, social, political, and national demands of the Negro masses, but 'especially the agrarian demands of the Negro farmers and tenants of the South.'"[30] N. Nasonov wrote an article reemphasizing the national aspect of African American oppression and criticized the Party's previous position. Quoting John Reed comments at the Second Comintern Congress (cited above), that African Americans "feel at home" in the United States, Nasonov rhetorically asked, "Since when has John Reed, a talented artist of the October Revolution, become the exponent of the yearnings of the Negroes?"[31] Invoking the authority of Lenin, Nasonov concluded that "Lenin referred many times to the Negroes as an oppressed nation, and, what is more interesting, Lenin refers to the Negroes often when speaking about Ireland."[32] Harry Haywood also contributed several articles in the early 1930's.[33]

The articles cited above show that the Party actively campaigned to educate the membership to see the importance of the African American struggle and to urge their participation in it. The constant polemics about viewing the African American question as a national question rather than as a race question was an attempt to break with the Socialist Party pattern. In short, what the party was attempting to do was to create a political culture within the CPUSA that would have zero tolerance for racism and would place the importance of the African American question near the top of the political agenda along with the class struggle.

The Party's intervention in the struggle of the African American people met with some success. They helped the defense of the Scottsboro defendants, organized steel workers in Birmingham, and led the struggle to organize share croppers in Alabama struggle. In the North they became active in the straggle for the integration of neighborhoods, and against employment discrimination.

---

[29] Joseph Prokopec, "Negroes As an Oppressed National Minority." *The Communist*. March 1930, 9(3), 244–245. B.D. Amis makes a similar point in "For a Strict Leninist Analysis on the Negro Question." *The Communist*, October 1932, 14(10), 944–949. Amis notes, "To maintain that the Negro question is a 'race question,' or that the oppression of Negroes is based upon the 'color line' is to blur over its social and economic essence; in other words, to capitulate to bourgeois race theories."

[30] Prokopec, 244–245.

[31] N. Nasonov, "Against Liberalism in the American Negro Question," *The Communist*, April 1930, 9(4), 307.

[32] Nasonov, 308.

[33] See "Against Bourgeois-Liberal Distortions of Leninism on the Negro Question in the United States." *The Communist*, August 1930, 9(8), 649–712 and "The Struggle for the Leninist Position on the Negro Question in the U.S.A.," *The Communist*, Septermber 1933, 12(9), 888–901.

Recently there has developed a new scholarship of the early civil rights movement that sheds much light on communist participation in the African American struggle.[34] However, scholars writing on the issue of the communist's call for the right of self-determination have nearly unanimously agreed that the Comintern position had no practical utility.[35]

That is only accurate if the slogan of self-determination is artificially separated from the demands for the redistribution of land. First, it must be remembered that two of the principle activities of the Party in the South during the 1930's was organizing workers in industry and organizing tenant farmers. The organizing of tenant farmers was a necessary precursor to the demand for the confiscation of plantation lands, which the Party believed was a necessary prerequisite to any serious consideration of implementing the right to self-determination. Secondly, the only way to initiate the fight for agrarian reform was to begin to organize tenant farmers around day-to-day survival issues.

In a 1932 speech printed in *The Communist*, party leader Earl Browder attempted a summation of the party's activities among African Americans:

> In the midst of the Scottsboro campaign we made another political step forward, in the struggle of the Negro sharecroppers in Camp Hill [Alabama]. This battle was the first struggle directly resulting from our penetration of the Black Belt, of the agrarian population. It brought out the basic question of the Negroes as a nation, the question of land and land-tenure, the question of the agrarian revolution, the overthrowing of the semi-feudal agrarian relationships. While immediately Camp Hill was only a struggle for certain partial demands, and correctly so, it threw a bright light upon the basic problem of the land, and thereby became a political milestone in the development of our Negro work.[36]

Unfortunately, there has been no major study of the Alabama Share Cropper's Union.[37] An early article by John Beecher does suggest there may be more of a link between self-determination and mass organizing. Beecher quotes an article from the 1933 *Birmingham World*, an African American paper, in which the reporter comments: "Meetings were held in houses. Sometimes literature was distributed. Self-determination of the Black Belt was mentioned at the meetings. Nobody knew very much about the details of the idea,

---

[34] See Martha Biondi's *To Stand and Fight: The Struggle for Civil Rights in Postwar New York City* (Cambridge, MA: Harvard University Press, 2003) and Robert Korstadt's *Civil Rights Unionism: Tobacco Workers and the Struggle for Democracy in the Mid-twentieth Century South* (Chapel Hill, University of North Carolina Press, 2003).

[35] See Mark Naison, *Communists in Harlem during the Depression* (Urbana: University of Illinois Press, 1983), 17–19 and Harvey Klehr and William Thompson. "Self-Determination in the Black Belt: origins of a Communist policy," *Labor History*, 30, 1989, 366.

[36] Earl Browder, "For National Liberation of the Negroes! War Against White Chauvinism!" *The Communist*, April 1932, 11(4), 299.

[37] Robin Kelley's *Hammer and Hoe* (Chapel Hill, University of North Carolina Press, 1990), includes a chapter on the Share Cropper's Union. However, like most other historians, he alleges "The slogan demanding self-determination in the black belt did not inspire Birmingham's nascent communist cadre to initiate a rural-based radical movement," 37–38.

folks in Tallapoosa County say, but all were eager to work for a chance to escape from poverty and fear."[38]

Perhaps future studies of the Share Cropper's Union and analyses of the *Southern Worker*, the CPUSA regional newspaper, will shed more light on this era and bring us to a clearer understanding of how the CPUSA's theoretical positions affected its practical work. What is clear is that knowledge of communist strategy and tactics, i.e., understanding the relationship of agitation on the right to self-determination to day-to-day organizing around immediate needs is crucial to understanding communist activities and the relationship between communist theory and practice.

Spurred on by the notion that African Americans had the right to determine their own destiny, were entitled to equality under the law, and by an unshakeable belief in interracial solidarity, the Communist Party entered Southern politics in the 1930's. They entered a region of the country that seemed not to have noticed that the South lost the Civil War. African Americans were wantonly murdered for even advocating an assertion of their Constitutional rights, with their abusers never having to fear punishment. The lives of whites who advocated equality were just as precarious. So inextricably connected were the notions of "communists" and "racial equality" in the white Southern consciousness that thirty years later, when the modern civil rights movement erupted, most Southern whites – and many non-Southern whites – were convinced it was a "communist plot."

Yet this lawless area was the terrain in which James and Esther Jackson and their colleagues chose to stand and fight. Inspired by the then-radical ideas of racial equality and justice they struggled to build a movement that – in the long run – helped to transform U.S. society. That so many of the ideas they stood for and the vision they projected have now become largely non-controversial is a testament to their ambition, work and life.

---

[38] John Beecher, "The Share Croppers' Union in Alabama," *Social Forces* 13 (1, 1934), 127.

Civil Rights Unionism and the Black Freedom Struggle

ROBERT KORSTAD

Historical writing on the civil rights movement is in the midst of a remarkable renaissance. Recently, at a conference of oral historians in Little Rock there were multiple sessions focused on what the historian Jacquelyn Hall has dubbed "the Long Civil Rights Movement." Many of these sessions dealt with struggles that came after the 1960s—these represented an extension of the movement to the present—but the concept of a Long Civil Rights Movement also looks back from the 1960s and it is that phase that I want to discuss.

Most historians would agree that the modern civil rights movement did not begin with the Supreme Court's decision in *Brown v. Board of Education.* Yet all too often the movement's history has been written as if events before the mid-1950s constituted a kind of prehistory, important only insofar as they laid the legal and political foundation for the spectacular advances that came later. Those were the "forgotten years of the Negro Revolution," wrote one historian; they were the "seed time of racial and legal metamorphosis," according to another. But such a periodization I would argue profoundly underestimates the tempo and misjudges the social dynamic of the freedom struggle.

The civil rights era began, dramatically and decisively, in the late 1930s when the social structure of black America took on an increasingly urban, proletarian character. A predominantly southern rural and small-town population was soon transformed into one of the most urban of all major ethnic groups. More than two million blacks migrated to northern and western industrial areas during the 1940s, while another million moved from farm to city within the South. Northern black voters doubled their numbers between 1940 and 1948, and in the eleven states of the Old South black registration more than quadrupled, reaching over one million by 1952. Likewise, membership in the National Association for the Advancement of Colored People (NAACP) soared, going from 50,000 in 355 branches in 1940 to almost 450,000 in 1000 branches by 1946.

The half million black workers who joined unions affiliated with the Congress of Industrial Organizations (CIO) were in the vanguard of efforts to transform race relations. The NAACP and the Urban League had become more friendly toward labor in the depression era, but their legal and social work orientation had not prepared them to act effectively in the workplaces and working-class neighborhoods where black Americans fought their most decisive struggles of the late 1930s and 1940s. By the early forties it was commonplace for sympathetic observers to assert the centrality of mass unionization in the civil rights struggle. A Rosenwald Fund study concluded, not without misgivings, that "the characteristic movements among Negroes are now for the first time becoming proletarian;" while a *Crisis* reporter found the CIO a "lamp of democracy" throughout the old Confederate states: "The South has not known such a force since the historic Union Leagues in the great days of the Reconstruction era."

This movement, which I call "Civil Rights Unionism," gained much of its dynamic character from the relationship that arose between unionized blacks and the federal government and proved somewhat similar to the creative tension that linked the church-based civil rights movement and the state almost two decades later. In the 1950s the Brown decision legitimated much of the subsequent social struggle, but it remained essentially a dead letter until given political force by a growing protest movement. In like manner, the rise of industrial unions and the evolution of late New Deal labor legislation offered working-class blacks an economic and political standard by which they could legitimate their demands and stimulate a popular struggle. The "one man, one vote" policy implemented in thousands of National Labor Relations Board (NLRB) elections, the industrial "citizenship" that union contracts offered once-marginal elements of the working class, and the patriotic egalitarianism of the government's wartime propaganda – all generated a rights consciousness that gave working-class black militancy a moral justification in some ways as powerful as that evoked by the Baptist spirituality of Martin Luther King, Jr., a generation later.

In the automobile factories of Detroit, the cotton presses of Memphis, the steel mills of Pittsburg and Birmingham, the shipyards of Baltimore and Detroit, and the tobacco factories of Richmond, Charleston, and Winston-Salem, the mobilization of black workers made civil rights an issue that could not be ignored by union officers, white executives, or government officials.

Civil Rights unionism represented a coming together of laborers, civil rights activists, progressive New Dealers, and black and white Radicals, some of whom were associated with the Communist Party. This was a national movement, with an engaged southern wing, and as such civil rights unionism was not a precursor of the modern civil rights movement, but its critical first phase. Many leaders, events, organizations come under the umbrella of civil rights unionism: the Double V campaign and A. Philip Randolph's March on Washington Movement.

Two other factors were critical to the broad social agenda: internationalism and left-labor feminism. African American activists were among the first to make the link between the Nazi persecution of the Jews and American racism. Likewise, the black working class drew strength from the emerging anti-colonial struggles and saw their struggle as part of an international fight for liberation. There was also a strong tie between civil rights unions and the left labor feminism that emerged in the 1940s. This was a broad movement that found its most articulate spokespeople in the Communist movement – whether it was Claudia Jones, Esther Cooper, or one of the heroines of my book, Moranda Smith. These leaders articulated a concept of the triple oppressive of black women because of race, class and gender.

By the mid-1940s, civil rights issues had reached a level of national political salience that they would not regain for another fifteen years. Once the domain of Afro-American protest groups, leftist clergymen, and Communist-led unions and front organizations, civil rights advocacy was becoming a defining characteristic of urban liberalism. Thus ten states established fair employment practice commissions between 1945 and 1950, and four major cities – Chicago, Milwaukee, Minneapolis, and Philadelphia – enacted tough laws against job bias. Backed by the CIO, the Americans for Democratic Action spearheaded a successful effort to strengthen the Democratic party's civil rights plank at the 1948 convention.

In the South the labor movement seemed on the verge of a major breakthrough. *Fortune* magazine predicted that the CIO's "Operation Dixie" would soon organize key southern industries like textiles. Black workers proved exceptionally responsive to such union campaigns, especially in industries like lumber, furniture, and tobacco, where they were sometimes a majority of the work force. Between 1944 and 1946 the CIO's political action apparatus helped elect liberal congressmen and senators in a few southern states, while organizations that promoted interracial cooperation, such as the Southern Conference for Human Welfare and Highlander Folk School, experienced their most rapid growth and greatest effectiveness in 1946 and 1947.

Yet, for all those accomplishments, civil rights unionism never realized its potential. Vicious anti-labor campaigns by American corporations forced strikes, and mechanization and automation caused thousands of workers to lose their jobs. Anti-communism was used to not only attack CP but the New Deal and Fair Deal social welfare reforms.

The collapse of civil rights unionism cast a long shadow over the second half of the twentieth century. The disintegration of the movements of the Popular Front era ensured that when the civil rights struggle of the 1960s emerged it would have a different social character and a different political agenda, which in the end proved inadequate to the immense social problems that lay before it. Like the workers' movement of the 1940s, the protests of the 1960s mobilized an African-American community that was overwhelmingly working-class. The key institutions of the new movement, however, were not the trade unions, but the black church and independent protest organizations. As Martin Luther

King, Jr, and others well knew, winning the vote and ending discrimination in public accommodations and education could not overturn the forces that impoverished African Americans. After 1965, such activists sought to raise issues of economic equality and working-class empowerment to the moral high ground occupied by the assault on disfranchisement and segregation. Yet they found themselves hamstrung by the institutional and cultural rifts between civil rights and labor, the divisions between the haves and have nots within the working class. Most important perhaps, they could not build on the alternative social vision of the 1940s, for that vision had been lost to memory to a large extent, destroyed by the political repression of the McCarthy era.

There were other repercussions as well, for the South, for labor, for the women's movement, and for American political culture. The South has prospered in ways that the activists of the 1940s could never have imagined or foreseen, but it still suffers from its historical reluctance to invest in health, education, and other dimensions of "human capital." Just as leftists feared, conservative southern congressmen did help to push through an edifice of labor law that hampers the labor movement to this day. The South, along with reservoirs of even cheaper labor abroad, continues to lure runaway shops, ensuring that capital will retain the advantage of infinite mobility over labor. The CIO's embrace of Cold War ideology, its thralldom to the Democratic Party, and its attempt to forge a postwar "settlement" with leading corporations ended the industrial union project of the 1930s. The purge of the left-led unions deprived that movement of organizers oriented toward the heterogeneous workforce that would emerge after World War II. McCarthyism cut the women's liberation movement off from one strand of its history: the multi-ethnic left feminism represented by the women of the 1940s, leaving the movement vulnerable to the charge of being racially exclusive and middle-class. The list could go on. All the ills that beset America cannot be chalked up to the outcome of the struggles of the 1940s. But that outcome does stand as a watershed.

As the 21st century begins, the South and the North have yet to erase the color line, have yet to extend democratic citizenship to the workplace, have yet to attend to the basic health, education, and welfare needs of its most vulnerable citizens, have yet to create a truly participatory political system. Despite the enormous changes of the past 50 years, which are the results of this long civil rights movement, the persistence of the past is everywhere apparent. Perhaps only when another generation of activists refashion the dreams of the 1940s to fit the contours of the new century will the legacy of racial capitalism be laid to rest.

Lorraine Hansberry's Freedom Family

MICHAEL ANDERSON

Lorraine Hansberry and the periodical *Freedom* both appeared in New York City in November 1950, and soon would be united in a marriage of true minds. Hansberry, as she would recall, was "twenty-one & confused and stifled inside"[1] when she wandered into "a somewhat bare and harrowed Harlem office overlooking Lenox Avenue. An office furnished with two desks, one typewriter and a remarkably enthusiastic working staff of two,"[2] the office manager, Edith Roberts, and the editor, Louis E. Burnham. Hansberry knew she had found safe harbor. "I work for the new Negro paper, FREEDOM, which in its time in history ought to be *the* journal of Negro liberation . . . in fact, it will be,"[3] she proclaimed shortly after joining the staff (at a weekly salary of $31.70) to work "as subscription clerk, receptionist, typist and editorial assistant,"[4] a job description Burnham published under the headline "In the Freedom Family."

For once a journalistic cliché reveals a deeper truth. What Hansberry found during the two years she worked full-time at *Freedom* was nurture. The people she met, the expanded range of progressive politics, the workaday routine, and, perhaps most of all, the knowledge that there were other people just as committed to a politics of liberation and an aesthetic of community, that to live such a life was possible, that, as she would put it, "the future is mine to do whatever I choose"[5] – this was the incubator for Hansberry's transition from activist to artist, from a dedicated foot soldier of the Communist Party to the internationally celebrated artistic foremother of contemporary human-rights movements.

Recalling her time at the publication, Hansberry wrote: "There is something beyond the concept of a 'job' which makes the *Freedom* people work so hard

---

[1] Lorraine Hansberry, undated fragment, Hansberry Archive, Schomburg Center for Research into Black Culture, New York Public Library (hereafter Hansberry Archive).

[2] Lorraine Hansberry, "Freedom's first struggling 3 years — a proud record," *People's World*, February 4, 1954, Hansberry Archive.

[3] Lorraine Hansberry, *To Be Young, Gifted and Black: Lorraine Hansberry in Her Own Words*, adapted by Robert Nemiroff (New York: Vintage Books, 1995), 77.

[4] Publicity handout for the musical *Raisin*, Hansberry Archive; (Louis E. Burnham), "In the Freedom Family," *Freedom*, Sept., 1951, 2.

[5] Hansberry, undated fragment, Hansberry Archive.

to achieve so much with so very little.[6] When introducing her to *Freedom's* readership, Burnham had noted that in addition to Hansberry's clerical duties (before her rapid promotion to associate editor), "in between she finds time to write fine poetry and an occasional article."[7] No sooner had she joined *Freedom*, which had been founded by Paul Robeson as part of his tightening embrace of the Communist Party line in the increasingly frigid Cold War, than she was serving as a participant-correspondent: she accompanied the "Sojourners for Truth and Justice," a group of 132 black women from 15 states which was convened in September 1951, in Washington by the long-time activist Mary Church Terrell "to demand that the Federal Government protect the lives and liberties"[8] of black Americans. Hansberry's full-page report detailed the graphic and, inevitably, frustrating encounter between officials of the Justice Department and women like Amy Mallard, the widow of a World War II veteran who had been shot to death for attempting to vote in Georgia.[9] Likewise, Hansberry traveled to Mississippi with a delegation of women bearing petitions seeking a commutation of the death sentence given to Willie McGee, a black man convicted of raping a white woman. McGee was executed on May 8, 1951, inspiring perhaps the best of Hansberry's attempts at poetry, "Lynchsong," published in *Masses & Mainstream* in July 1951:

> Laurel:
> > Name sweet like the breath of peace
>
> > Blood and blood
> > Hatred there
> > White robes and
> > Black robes
> > And a burning
> > Burning cross
> > > cross in Laurel
> > > cross in Jackson
> > > cross in Chicago
> > And a
> > Cross in front of the City Hall
> > In:
> > New York City
>
> > Lord
> > Burning cross
> > Lord
> > Burning man
> > Lord
> > Murder cross

---

[6] Hansberry, "Freedom's first struggling years — a proud record," *op. cit.*

[7] "In the Freedom Family," *op. cit.*

[8] Robert Nemiroff, "From These Roots: Lorraine Hansberry and the South," *Southern Exposure,* September/October, 1984, 33; Lorraine Hansberry, "Women Voice Demands in Capital Sojourn", *Freedom,* Oct. 1951, 6; *Daily Worker,* October 1, 1951, 8, quoted in Document NY 100-107297, 10, of Lorraine Hansberry (HQ 100-393031), Federal Bureau of Investigation.

[9] Nemiroff, "From These Roots," 33–34.

Laurel:
Name bitter like the rhyme of a lynchsong

I can hear Rosalie
See the eyes of Willie McGee
My mother told me about
Lynchings
My mother told me about
The dark nights
And dirt roads
And torch lights
And lynch robes
   sorrow nights
   and a
   sorrow night
The
Faces of men
Laughing white
Faces of men
Dead in the night
   sorrow night
   and a
   sorrow night[10]

Certainly, the most dramatic of Hansberry's exploits in advocacy journalism came in March 1952, when she stood proxy for Robeson as one of five American delegates to the Inter-American Peace Conference in Montevideo, Uruguay. Two years earlier, Robeson's passport had been voided on the grounds, in the words of Ruth Shipley, the right-wing termagant who held the State Department's passport office hostage from 1928 to 1955, that "Robeson's travel abroad at this time would be contrary to the best interests of the United States." This restriction would hold until 1958 when the U.S. Supreme Court ruled, 5–4, that passports could not be denied on political grounds. (It is a measure of Robeson's prominence that such travel restrictions remain in force on him long after they had been removed for members of the national committee of the Communist Party USA).[11]

But in 1952 Robeson was grounded; and Hansberry took his place among the 250 delegates from Communist peace organizations in Paraguay, Brazil, Venezuela, Argentina, Puerto Rico, Chile, Colombia, Uruguay and the United States[12] (one of whom was Salvadore Allende[13]). Perhaps the high point for Hansberry came when she presented the American delegation's gift to the host committee. "In my hand," she said, "I hold a message from a man whose name in our country is synonymous with the word peace." "As the translator got out this much," she reported, "the ovation broke." A crowd she estimated at 5,000

---

[10] Lorraine Hansberry, "Lynchsong," *Masses & Mainstream*, July 1951, 20.

[11] Robert L. Beisner, *Dean Acheson: A Life in the Cold War* (New York: Oxford University Press, 2006), p. 114; quoted in Martin Duberman, *Paul Robeson* (New York: Alfred A. Knopf, 1988), 389, 463, 451.

[12] Lorraine Hansberry, "'Illegal Conference' Shows Peace is the Key to Freedom," *Freedom*, April 1952, 3.

[13] Lorraine Hansberry, untitled speech, Hansberry Archives.

FIG. 1. **Lorraine Hansberry (left) with Eliza Brenco at the Inter-American Congress for Peace at Montevideo, Uruguay, March 1952.** *Daily Worker* **photography morgue, reproduced with permission of the Communist Party USA.**

began to cheer: "Viva Robeson!"[14] She would describe this experience in the articles and speeches upon her return to New York, which gave her remarkable prominence in Communist circles. (The best summary, less articulate than her public utterances, but all the more heartfelt, may be found in a letter she wrote from Montevideo: "The peace forces all over the world may well be proud and enheartened by the efforts of the peoples of the Americas to confer for peace. ... we who are American have a [*sic*] overwhelming responsibility to the world _ gosh _ overwhelming."[15]) At the time, Hansberry was about six weeks shy of her twenty-second birthday.

She carried a considerable political resumé when she had arrived in New York, at the age of twenty. Lorraine Hansberry was born into activism. Her parents, who had moved to Chicago from Tennessee and Mississippi during to the Great Migration and, atypically, who both had been

---

[14] Hansberry, "'Illegal Conference' Shows Peace is the Key to Freedom".

[15] Lorraine Hansberry, no date, typewritten letter on stationery reading "Palacio Florida Hotel, Montevideo," Hansberry Archive.

college-educated, had been energetic members of Chicago's black Republican machine, which had been so successful at placing jobholders in the administration of Mayor "Big Bill" Thompson that City Hall had earned the nickname "Uncle Tom's Cabin."[16] (Lorraine's mother had been a GOP ward committee woman, her father a Federal marshal: "I recall being the *only* child in my classes who did not come from the Rooseveltian atmosphere of the homes of the thirties,"[17] she wrote.) Her father, a very well-to-do businessman, had been a financial backer and officer of the Chicago branch of the NAACP and the Chicago Urban League. Moreover, Lorraine, like her two older brothers and sister, had been taught that "Above all, there were two things which were never to be betrayed: the family and the race."[18] Accordingly, her eldest brother fought induction into the Jim Crow Army during World War II; and her sister found herself spending her prom night nervously sitting with her date in a restaurant suspected of mistreating black patrons.

Not surprisingly, Lorraine's first act upon entering the University of Wisconsin was to integrate one of its living units. "She was the only girl I knew who could whip together a fresh picket sign with her own hands, at a moment's notice, for any cause or occasion," Hansberry's classmate at Wisconsin, the future broadcast journalist Bob Teague wrote. "She spent every spare moment away from the classrooms trying to change it, working with student action groups."[19] Lorraine promptly joined the Young Progressives of America; she would become president of the organization in her sophomore year and worked on Henry Wallace's presidential campaign. "I recall that you were slightly skeptical of Mr. Wallace's abilities in spite of his intentions," she wrote that summer of 1948 to a college friend, "— and at such time I agreed — however, in light of present situations I have gone 100% Progressive.... things are bad Edythe. A lot worse than we realize I'm afraid — for instance, here in Chicago a district Police Chief made public a statement declaring that *any mixed meeting* (in his eyesight) anywhere in the City *constitute Communist gatherings.*"[20]

Such activity did not meet with the approval of Hansberry's widowed mother; in another letter to her college chum, she wrote: "My family has *forbidden* my attending so much as *one* more Wallace meeting — I am quite sick about it. They are afraid Little Lorraine will call up one night from the Police Station and ask for her pajamas or tied to a post with a [hammer and sickle]

[16] Harold F. Gosnell, *Negro Politicians: The Rise of Negro Politics in Chicago* (Chicago: The University of Chicago Press, 1935), 55; St. Clair Drake and Horace R. Cayton, *Black Metropolis: A Study of Negro Life in a Northern City* (New York: A Harbinger Book/Harcourt, Brace & World, 1945), Vol. I, 348.

[17] Lorraine Hansberry, "Memoirs," 3, Hansberry Archive. Emphasis Hansberry's.

[18] *Ibid.*, 6.

[19] Bob Teague, *Letters to a Black Boy* (New York: Lancer Books, 1969), 45.

[20] Lorraine Hansberry to Edythe Cohen, July 31, 1948, xerox copy, Hansberry Archive. Ellipsis mine; emphasis, capitalization and punctuation, Hansberry's.

branded on my forehead by a local 'patriots' _ ... I am sincerely interested in what I have been doing — and because I felt that I was *doing something*."[21]

It was also in Madison, on January 7, 1950, that Hansberry attended a Communist recruitment party.[22] Apparently she did not join the Party until later in the year, after she abandoned her college studies and moved to New York, where she almost immediately was a presence on picket lines, tenants' protests and as a street-corner orator, where, an acquaintance remembered, "she spoke with the fierceness of a young Harriet Tubman."[23] Such activity would continue; for example, Hansberry was on the faculty when the Frederick Douglass Educational Center opened; she taught an evening class in "Public Speaking for Progressives" she worked in local campaigns for candidates of the People's Rights Party and the American Labor Party; she participated in the Jefferson School's Sunday forums, conducting readings and discussions on topics like "Working Class Poets of the Negro People"[24] (also at Jefferson she took a seminar on Africa given by W.E.B. Du Bois): she worked several summers on the staff of Camp Unity; and, in the three years after she left *Freedom*, she would serve as associate editor and write numerous articles for the Communist magazine for young people *New Challenge*. However, it was at *Freedom* that Hansberry gained not so much direction as focus. It was there that she gained what she sought in leaving the University of Wisconsin, "education of another kind."[25] The abrasions to her sensibility from a range of progressive activities, as grand as her trip to South America, as nitty-gritty as marching on a picket line, both grounded her commitment to a materialist interpretation of history and social change, and increasingly caused her to be, as she wrote at the time, "obsessed with a rather desperate desire for a new world for me and my brothers." (She added: "So, dear friend, I must perhaps go to jail. Please at the next red-baiting session you hear ... remember this 'Communist.'"[26]).

She also gained the discipline, invaluable for a young writer, of having to produce under the pressure of deadline, of, very simply, being required to actually put words on paper, no small gift for a still somewhat spoiled upper-middle class girl, given to intermittent bursts of enthusiasm for poetry, drawing, journalism, fiction and play writing. As Beneatha Younger, the character

---

[21] Lorraine Hansberry to Edythe Cohen, postmarked August 9, 1948, xerox copy, Hansberry Archive. Ellipsis mine.

[22] Document MI 100-10902 in Lorraine Hansberry's files (HQ Cross-References), Federal Bureau of Investigation.

[23] Loyle Hairston, "Lorraine Hansberry—Portrait of an Angry Young Writer," *The Crisis*, April 1979, 123.

[24] Document CG 100-26009 in Lorraine Hansberry's files (HQ 100-393031), Federal Bureau of Investigation; *Counterattack*, February 4, 1955, 3, in Lorraine Hansberry's files (HQ Cross-References), Federal Bureau of Investigation; advertisement, *Daily Worker*, March 26, 1952, in Lorraine Hansberry's files (NY 100-107297, section 1), Federal Bureau of Investigation; advertisement from the *Daily Worker*, February 8, 1952, 8; Jefferson School Bulletin, No. 4 (week of February 4 [1952]), in Lorraine Hansberry's files (NY 100-107297, section 1), Federal Bureau of Investigation.

[25] Hansberry, *To Be Young, Gifted and Black*," 71.

[26] Lorraine Hansberry, draft for an unsent letter to Edythe Cohen, Hansberry Archive.

drawn as her self-portrait, would say in *A Raisin in the Sun*, "I don't flit! I – I experiment with different forms of expression."[27] (Eighteen months after that play's premiere, she made a list of "PROPOSED WORK" that listed five plays, a musical, an opera, a novel and "some short stories." She told an interviewer at this time: "I never could start anything other than, you know, the whole thing at one time and just - wham - into it. . . . I want to continue the process; I want to continue just tackling things and writing plays all the way out. . .)"[28] Fame would only exacerbate Hansberry's problem; she had "tremendous conflicts" about taking the necessary time from political activity to write.[29] Hansberry also suffered from the loneliness that afflicts most creative writers ("Eventually it comes to you: the things that makes you exceptional, if you are at all, is inevitably that which also must make you lonely"[30]), which may be why she especially enjoyed the communal nature of the theater. Carmen Capalbo, the first director of her second Broadway production, recalled her enthusiastic response to his criticisms of an early draft of *The Sign in Sidney Brustein's Window*: "Thank God! That's what I've been waiting to hear."[31] *A Raisin in the Sun* was developed over months in conversations, sometimes weekly, between Hansberry and the play's director, Lloyd Richards, who recalled: "She took the suggestion and the clarification of a point of view and if she accepted it, then she would find *her* way of doing it. . . . The solutions were very much hers."[32]

Freedom also introduced Hansberry to an enormous range of personalities, from Robeson and Du Bois to the hothouse of young black cultural workers, people like Alice Childress (a fellow *Freedom* staffer with whom Hansberry wrote her earliest surviving dramatic work, a pageant for the publication's Negro History Festival in 1952, which was narrated by Harry Belafonte[33]), Douglas Turner Ward, Sidney Poitier, and John O. Killens.

It was also while working at *Freedom*, covering a demonstration in 1951 protesting the exclusion of blacks from the basketball team at New York University, that she met one of the protestors, Robert Nemiroff, whom she would marry two years later and who would become the bedrock of support for her artistic activities for the rest of her life and the guardian of her legacy, following Hansberry's death from pancreatic cancer in 1965, at the age of thirty-four. Theirs was another marriage of true minds. Nemiroff was a postgraduate student in literature, was-as would become evident-passionate about

[27] Lorraine Hansberry, *A Raisin in the Sun: A Drama in Three Acts*, New York: Random House, 1959, Act I, Scene 1, 32.

[28] Hansberry, *To Be Young, Gifted and Black*, 125.

[29] "INTERVIEW — ROBERT NEMIROFF by Catherine Scheader, 8/1/76," typescript, 40, Hansberry Archives.

[30] Hansberry, *To Be Young, Gifted and Black*, 137.

[31] Michael Anderson, interview with Carmen Capalbo, September 28, 1999.

[32] Michael Anderson, interview with Lloyd Richards, October 12, 1999. This method of creative collaboration with the playwright was one Richards would follow for the rest of his distinguished career, most notably with August Wilson.

[33] Lorraine Hansberry and Alice Childress, "NEGRO HISTORY FESTIVAL: February 29, 1952," Hansberry Archives.

the theater (after the success *of A Raisin in the Sun* he would start a production company to mount Hansberry's works and wrote a musical version of *A Raisin in the Sun* that was produced on Broadway in 1973) and was a dedicated member of the Communist Party. He and Lorraine spent the day before their wedding in Chicago marching in a picket line to protest the execution of the Rosenbergs. "We spent Saturday night picketing the courthouse in Chicago and we were married on Sunday," Nemiroff recalled. "And they were executed Saturday night. And we had no heart for the wedding. I mean, we had heart for the wedding, but..."[34] Hansberry's own, somewhat dramatized account (Nemiroff said she "wrote notes on what might have become a short story, except that it never did"[35]) reads in part:

> We had come to a wedding. We had come to Chicago to lose our selves in the Bridal Song...And then there were those moments when the news came. And we spoke of it quietly to one another-our voices soft under the discussion of where the cake would be placed and when the photographers would arrive, and who must adjust the Bridal [*sic*] train. Our voices above the champagne glasses, our eyes questioning one another between the fresh fragrant flowers in their gleaming pots on the coffee tables of the wedding house, festive house. The Chicago heat in the vast living room suddenly overpowering the senses, some grim terrible fire within suddenly making it more awful, more stifling-the desire to fling the glass into the flowers, to thrust one's arms into the air and run out of the house screaming at ones [*sic*] countrymen to come down out of the apartments, down from the houses, to get up from the television sets, from the dinner tables, from the kitchens where the dishes were being washed with the evening time conversation – someone makes a hurried phone call to the committee to find out where the Line [*sic*] will be. We realize it is the bridegroom wearing the shiny new wedding clothes, and damp warm perspiration, he talks to the committee. The bride sits a moment in a corner alone to herself – she thinks:
>   And what shall I say to my children? And how shall I explain such a thing to them?[36]

But Hansberry's greatest gift from *Freedom* was her association with Louis Burnham. This "commanding personality,"[37] as she called him, the former executive secretary of the Southern Negro Youth Congress who had crossed swords with "Bull" Connor in Birmingham, Alabama, fifteen years before that name became internationally infamous,[38] was as kind-hearted as he was committed. "I told him of the novel I wanted to write," Hansberry recalled, "how I was desperately worried about having become too jaded, at twenty, to retain all the lovely things I had wanted to say in my novel when I was eighteen. It was part of his genius as a human being that he did not laugh or

---

[34]"INTERVIEW — ROBERT NEMIROFF by Catherine Scheader, 8/1/76," 15.

[35] *Ibid.*

[36] Lorraine Hansberry, "A Memorial — in Three Parts: June 1952," 8–9, Hansberrry Archives. Ellipsis mine; capitalization and punctuation Hansberry's.

[37] Hansberry, *To Be Young, Gifted and Black*, 79.

[38] Diane McWhorter, *Carry Me Home: Birmingham, Alabama: The Climactic Battle of the Civil Rights Revolution* (New York: Simon & Schuster, 2001), 58.

patronize my dilemma, but went on to gently and seriously prod me to consider the possibilities of the remaining time of my life."[39] The desire to be a creative writer had been burning within Hansberry at least since adolescence, camouflaged by her announced intention (as in her high school yearbook[40]) to become a journalist. However, Hansberry had made an appearance as a writer two months before she arrived in New York City: her poem "Flag From a Kitchenette Window" had been published in *Masses & Mainstream*.[41] It was Burnham who "encouraged her to take her fledgling efforts as a playwright seriously," Nemiroff wrote, and "Hansberry's first publicly produced dramatic works were staged at *Freedom* events"[42]: a pageant that "unfolded the history of the Negro newspaper in America and its fighting role in the struggle for a people's freedom, from 1827 to the birth of FREEDOM," and a pageant, directed by Julian Mayfield and staged at a "Cultural Salute to Paul Robeson" in 1954.[43]

This mixture of political purpose and artistic aspiration fueled Hansberry when she devoted herself to full-time playwriting ("All which I feel I must write has become obsessive. So many truths seem to be rushing at me as a result of things felt and seen and lived through. Oh what I think I must tell this world. Oh the time I crave — and the peace — and the *power*")[44] in 1956, three years after she left *Freedom*. She was able to do so thanks to the popular singer Eddie Fisher, who had a massive hit recording of a folk song adapted by her husband, "Cindy Oh Cindy." Later that year she began writing *A Raisin in the Sun*.[45] In that play can be found many of the themes she had pondered during the decade, like a critique of consumer capitalism (think of Walter exclaiming, "Hell, yes, I want me some yachts someday! Yes, I want to hang some real pearls 'round my wife's neck"[46]) – feminist advocacy, as in Beneatha's seriocomic efforts to establish an identity, and a discussion of colonial liberationist politics in Africa, in the dialogues of Beneatha and Assagai. More profound than this, of course, is the depth and breadth of characterizations, the play's extraordinary felt humanity – the element that led to the play's astounding success (not only in the United States: within two years, *A Raisin in the Sun* had been translated into thirty-five languages, and was being produced as far away as Tokyo, where the actors wore blackface). That is why the play retains its status as the most widely taught work of black literature; but in 1959, when it premiered, *A Raisin in the Sun* had its

---

[39] Hansberry, *To Be Young, Gifted and Black*, 79.

[40] Lorraine Hansberry, "Flag from a Kitchenette Window," *Masses & Mainstream*, Vol. 3, No. 9 (September, 1950), 38–40. As the identification line noted, this was Hansberry's first published work.

[41] Hansberry, *To Be Young, Gifted and Black*, 42.

[42] Nemiroff, *From These Roots*, 34.

[43] "In the Freedom Family," *Freedom*, December 1951, 3; "Topical Show to Salute Robeson, *Daily Worker*, May 25, 1954, 2, included with Document 100-411193-3 in Lorraine Hansberry's files (HQ Cross-References), Federal Bureau of Investigation.

[44] Lorraine Hansberry, "Chicago – Christmas 1955," Hansberry Archives. Emphasis Hansberry's.

[45] Henderson Cleaves, "People Get Messed Up, Says Author of 'Raisin,' " *New York World-Telegram and Sun*, March 13, 1959.

[46] Hansberry, *A Raisin in the Sun*, Act III, 133.

most significant domestic impact in its assault on white racist perceptions. It truly laid the groundwork for, almost exactly a year later, the four college freshmen at North Carolina A&T who sat down at a lunch counter in Greensboro, North Carolina – and who would not be moved.

Hansberry had issued a challenge to herself when she began work on *A Raisin in the Sun* "I'm going to write a social drama about Negroes that will be good art."[47] Her great success arose from her uncanny combination of an articulate political passion and a no less passionate but equally compelling emotional urgency. *A Raisin in the Sun* is a domestic drama; it depicts the reconciliation of a family as each member recognizes and accepts a transcendent ethic. Moreover, the action of the play, and, ultimately, the source of its higher truth, is the father, who has died before the action of the play begins. Such is the template for each of the plays Hansberry worked on in the six years remaining to her. Every one of them is a family play; each depicts a family in an effort to reconstitute itself in the light of true principle, occasioned by the death of a father figure (in fact, all of Hansberry's plays subsequent to *A Raisin in the Sun* shows death as part of the on-stage action). No matter whether she is showing the conundrums of commitment in Greenwich Village (*The Sign in Sidney Brustein's Window*), the dynamics of the Civil War on an antebellum Southern plantation (*The Drinking Gourd*), the necessity of anti-colonialist revolt in Africa (*Les Blancs*) or the fate of humanity following nuclear apocalypse (*What Use Are Flowers?*), Hansberry always followed the same pattern: what happens in a family - on what basis can it achieve mutual respect and support - when the patriarchal order collapses?[48]

Hansberry's father, the impassioned civil rights fighter whom she adored - "my father's enduring image in my mind is that of a man who kings might have imitated," she wrote; "a man who always seemed to be doing something brilliant and/or unusual to such an extent that to be doing something brilliant and/or unusual was the way I assumed Fathers [*sic*] behaved[49] – died very suddenly of a cerebral hemorrhage two months before her sixteenth birthday. He died an embittered man. He had waged a legal fight against housing discrimination is Chicago, and even had won a case in the United States Supreme Court, but the results of that decision proved far less decisive than had

---

[47] Nan Robertson, "Dramatist Against the Odds," *The New York Times*, March 8, 1959, Arts & Leisure section, p. 3.

[48] Hansberry's other projects, unfinished and unpublished, also follow this pattern, such as a film adaptation of Charles W. Chestnutt's *The Marrow of Tradition*, which is concerned with two families, one white and one black, in the antebellum South. Robert Nemiroff also recalls that one of the plays Hansberry attempted before *A Raisin in the Sun*, called *Final Glory*, concerning a union organizer, contains "one very, very moving scene in it, which is the relationship between the man that I'm talking about and his younger brother, who is a college student and he crosses the line to work": "INTERVIEW — ROBERT NEMIROFF by Catherine Scheader, 8/1/76," p. 19. Judith E. Smith presents a learned and compelling discussion of this theme *in A Raisin in the Sun*, which she views as the culmination of artistic representations that both documented and accelerated the democratization of American society following World War II, in *Visions of Belonging: Family Stories, Popular Culture, and Postwar Democracy, 1940–1960* (New York: Columbia University Press, 2004), 281–327.

[49] Hansberry, "Memoirs," 2, 3.

been hoped. "American racism helped kill him,"[50] she told interviewers two decades later, and the emotional devastation of her father's death spurred her to pick up his fight, to carry it forward - all the more because she perceived her mother, her brothers and her sisters as *not* doing so, as preoccupying themselves with her father's business ventures and with making money ("the whole family is very materialistically inclined," Nemiroff commented,[51] and Lorraine's sister, Mamie, would remark a half-century after her father's death, "Hansberrys always have making money in the back of their mind[52]") rather than with the social advocacy of the Hansberry patriarch.

And yet, *A Raisin in the Sun* is dedicated to her mother, and it is to her mother that Lorraine wrote, on the eve of the play's first out-of-town tryout, "I hope it will make you very proud."[53] Home is that place where, when you have to go there, they have to take you in; and Lorraine Hansberry's life, in many ways, was devoted to working out how that home might be made comfortable. Having little taste and less use for the psychoanalytic,[54] Hansberry as artist could map a personal difficulty onto the world as social drama; she could illuminate that the human family is not merely a glib metaphor but the most stubborn of realities - all the more so in the shadow of Hiroshima and Auschwitz. And with the prescience of the artist, she put on the Broadway stage, immediately before a generation of young Americans would dramatize it for the entire country, that the American family - the same entity whether called "the beloved community" or "Black and White Unite and Fight" - would somehow have to learn what it is that could bind its members in healthy and honest relation.

The politics of Hansberry suggested the path to be followed; the art of Hansberry illuminated the human condition that transcends simplistic prescriptions. (Susan Sontag's comment, "Brecht's political attitudes are, at best, the occasion for his humanism. They allow him to focus and expand his drama"[55] is equally applicable to Hansberry.) Her ability to forge a valid and vibrant union of these two poles of her sensibility is in itself an example of familial nurturance. The personal conflicts she carried with her from Chicago would find their field of resolution in New York City, where she found the family that gave her freedom.

---

[50] "Talk of the Town," *The New Yorker*, May 9, 1959, 34.

[51] "INTERVIEW — ROBERT NEMIROFF by Catherine Scheader, 8/1/76," 23.

[52] Michael Anderson, interview with Mamie Hansberry, November 29, 2001.

[53] Lorraine Hansberry to Nannie Hansberry, January 19, 1959, Hansberry Archives; Hansberry, *To Be Young, Gifted and Black*, 91.

[54] See Lorraine Hansberry, "The Origin of Character," presented at the symposium "The creative use of the Unconscious" at the Eighth Annual Conference of the American Academy of Psychotherapists, October 5, 1963, Hansberry Archives; *Journal of American Academy of Psychotherapists*, 5 (1964), 13–17.

[55] Susan Sontag, "Ionesco," in *Against Interpretation* (New York: Anchor Books, 1990; orig. pub. 1966), 121.

James and Esther Jackson: Connecting the Past to the Present

ANGELA DAVIS

James and Esther Jackson have given us a magnificent legacy. Their papers will be in very good company at the Tamiment Library, sharing space with the papers of Elizabeth Gurley Flynn, Eugene Debs, the Abraham Lincoln Brigade, the Communist Party, and many other progressive individuals and organizations and movements. Researchers and activists will have the opportunity to explore these archives and discover important dimensions of the history of our country that have gone unrecorded: the history of the Left, the history of civil rights struggles, labor organizing, anti-racist organizing, and anti-war organizing.

I began by referring to the extraordinary legacy of James and Esther Jackson. How might we define "legacy" in this context? What is our relationship to the past? What are our negotiations through history? How do we manage different and sometimes conflicting temporalities? Legacy can be defined in two ways: one, a gift by law, especially of money or some personal property; two, something transmitted by or received from an ancestor or predecessor or from the past. In both instances there is an assumption that somehow the past is securely segregated from the present. Of course in law the originator of the legacy must first die in order for it to be transmitted.

Not all legacies, not all inheritances involve progress. I am currently teaching a course called "Theories of Slavery" which explores, among other things, the contemporary inheritances of slavery. The Thirteenth Amendment of the Constitution, in declaring that slavery and involuntary servitude were legally abolished, did not indicate how to define the object of abolition. That is to say, it doesn't tell us how slavery is to be defined. There is, of course, the clause allowing one exception to the abolition of slavery. However, even if we grant the exception and acknowledge that constitutionally-convicted persons are still relegated to a form of civil death related to the social death of slavery, we still have not understood all of the inheritances of slavery. As legal scholar Guyora Binder point out, the Thirteenth Amendment does not tell us precisely what features of slavery were to be abolished. He points out that the Thirteenth Amendment does not reveal whether it will abolish slavery in the sense that it converts human beings into property, whether it will abolish compulsory labor, corporal punishment, whether it will abolish non-citizenship, whether it will abolish social death or the "not-born" status of the slaves, that is, their lack of acknowledged kinship ties. The Thirteenth Amendment does not reveal whether it intends to abolish the racism that enables slavery. These observations about the ambiguity of the legislative abolition of slavery should help clarify why we can say that we live with many legacies of slavery today, including capital punishment, which is one of the more direct legacies of slavery. At the beginning of the twenty-first century, we can say that the project of abolition which W.E. B. Du Bois comprehensively discusses in *Black Reconstruction* has not yet been fully accomplished.

Some legacies are woven into the dominant narrative of the history of this country. Because discourses of progress and triumph are so closely linked the history of this country, the abolition of slavery is considered to be a major triumph over one of the more unfortunate aspects of U.S. history. Today it is assumed that slavery has been done away with and our lives unfold on the other side of that victory. The genocide of Native Americans and the regimes of racial segregation are also aspects of our past that are assumed to have been overcome. National legacies are wrought by declaring that the offending set of practices is now dead. Slavery is dead, segregation is dead, racism is dead. Consider how Rosa Park's legacy was celebrated in Washington. What was required in order for her to become the first woman whose body could lie in state in the vestibule of the Capitol? George Bush provided us with the answer to this question when he linked her legacy to what he represented as the ultimate triumph for democracy, not an ongoing struggle for democracy that continues to be waged today, but rather the triumph of a democracy that can be exported to Iraq and other places by means of violence and war.

The civil rights movement had to be declared dead in order for its legacies to be celebrated by the dominant culture. These legacies are also represented as individualized rather than collective. Individual figures, transformed into icons become the signs of these struggles. This iconization has a dangerous impact on the way we imagine radical movements, not to speak of the messiah effect it promotes for a leader who will take us over the mountain. In order for the figures of Martin Luther King, Rosa Parks Coretta Scott King, and others to be incorporated into a narrative about an unbroken quest for American democracy, their activism had to be declared over, dead.

On the other hand, there has been no attempt to assimilate the legacies of the Southern Negro Youth Congress into a triumphant narrative about American democracy. There has been no attempt to assimilate the legacies of the Communist Party, at least not explicitly, precisely because the legacies of James and Esther Jackson and those with whom they worked and struggled for so many decades, point to unfinished agendas of freedom. Such legacies that require continued struggle for democracy, freedom, and socialism could never be made to justify a so-called global war on terror. The Jacksons and their comrades fought and continue to fight for a freedom that could never be assimilated into a project of U.S. global domination through war and torture, through the wholesale denial of civil rights and human rights.

Speaking of legacies, the work of W.E.B. Du Bois has only recently begun to be broadly recognized. And, of course, we have in part David Levering Lewis to thank for that. But I have to admit that I'm sometimes a bit troubled – and I'm sure David Lewis has encountered similar situations – when academics (especially white academics, and those who had previously paid little attention to Black Studies) ã who have just learned about the work of Du Bois, assume that the Du Bois phenomenon is totally new. Moreover, if Du Bois's legacy is now being taken up in a much broader context than before, there are still dangerous aspects of that legacy that continue to remain subjugated. And there are a host of subjugated legacies associated with the lives and work of James and Esther Jackson, dangerous inheritances that might very well help us challenge and perhaps triumph over the U.S. drive for global empire.

The James and Esther Jackson papers may radically transform how we think about the history of the civil rights movement. One always looks for a dates to mark origins, and so there are several convenient origin dates. Sometimes *we use the Brown v. Board of Education* (1954) case to mark the beginning of the twentieth century black freedom movement. Sometimes we use the year 1955 because the Montgomery bus boycott started in December of that year. And then sometimes we use the date 1951 because of the "We Charge Genocide" petition that Paul Robeson and William L. Patterson presented to the United Nations.

When I think SNCC, instead of thinking Student Nonviolent Coordinating Committee, I think Southern Negro Youth Congress. So we have two SNCC's "SNICKS" – a SNCC and a SNYC. What we might call the Communist formation of those who worked with the Southern Negro Youth Congress, the formation both in and outside the Party allowed them to think about the black freedom struggle in terms that were never limited to the rather narrow legal freedom that eventually came to be hailed as the triumph of the civil rights movement. James and Esther Jackson and their comrades in SNYC never confused their visions of freedom with the so-called freedom that finds its most appropriate expression in the freedom of the capitalist market. They understood the ideological trick that makes it appear that for those who possess no capital, they do, at least, possess the freedom to sell their labor power.

The aim of James and Esther Jackson and of their comrades in the SNYC was not to insure that black people and other racially-oppressed communities would only achieve a limited freedom before the law, the freedom to appear as individual, abstract, rights-bearing subjects before the law. They fought for substantive freedoms, for labor rights, for the right to health care, not simply for formalistic equality before the law. Their strategies would never, for example, justify the incarceration of 2.2 million people who are currently in prison by the so-called equal treatment they all receive.

The Jacksons did not separate civil rights from labor rights. The freedom they wanted would entail vast revolutionary transformations. If James Jackson and the Southern Negro Youth Congress fought so hard for the unionization of tobacco workers, it was because they knew that people need to exercise collective rights. They also need to see these collective rights as guaranteeing the right to struggle, not only for individual rights but for revolutionary transformations, for socialism.

Their legacy could never be incorporated into the concept of "diversity" that now are offered to us as a contemporary way of addressing problems of race, class, gender and sexuality that we now confront. It is very distressing that this term diversity has colonized so much of what we were once able to talk about with a much greater degree of historical specificity,

I return to the more than 2.2 million people who are in prison. The U.S. incarcerates both absolutely and proportionately more people than any other country in the world. My niece Eisa Davis is performing in a musical called *Passing Strange*. There is a striking moment in the musical where one of the characters – a German anarchist humorously says "I want to be re-incarcerated as a black man." Jokes aside, we need to reconsider the extent to which the institution of the prison has become a kind of symbol of the democracy the U.S. is offering to the world. There are the military prisons—-and Abu Ghraib and Guantanamo, for example, and the many secret CIA prisons that are places of torture. But there is also the fact that U.S.-style prisons have followed structural readjustment in countries in the southern regions that are extremely poor. In areas of Africa where neocolonial conditions produce housing that is not fit for human beings, where conditions of extreme poverty define people's lives, you will find a new, sophisticated, technologically-developed prison as a place to deposit the expendable populations that are created by the influx of global capital.

My relationship to the Jacksons is not a scholarly relationship. My relationship to the Jacksons is personal and political. And in thinking about my connection with them over the years, I realize that I cannot undo the entanglement of the personal and the political.

I found in this wonderful pamphlet from the era of their youth an excerpt from a letter that Esther quoted, a letter from Jack written on the stationery of the Tobacco Stemmers and Laborers Industrial Union, which Jack had helped to organize at the export factory of the British-American Tobacco Company in Richmond, while Esther was still at Fisk. Let me read the passage. "Already," Jack writes, "I have missed the glorious Fisk hospitality, and most especially your contribution to the joyous stay I had there." "Of all the happy memories of my acquaintance with you will stand out in bold outline: a native unselfishness, a will to serve and to sacrifice, an ardent devotion to our cause symbolized in the youthful beauty of a charming lady."

This was passion, personal and political passion, so entirely intertwined with each other that it would have been impossible to separate the personal from the political. I think about the extent to which Esther and Jack and all of their

FIG. 1. Sallye Bell, mother of Angela Davis, from the 3rd Southern Negro Youth Conference Souvenir Program, 1939.

friends and comrades—-Dorothy Burnham, Louis Burnham, the Strongs, my mother Sallye Bell, who were involved in the organizing of the Southern Negro Youth Congress were totally driven by this personal/political passion. I think about their devotion, the way in which they took seriously the *zeitgeist of* the era and quite literally shaped the times with their organizing and political work. Esther and Jack gave up promising professional careers in order to devote themselves full time to the revolution. And although they were not unique among their generation, their decision to become organizers inspired others. Young people today need to know that they can follow their passions, and that they can be passionate about revolutionary change, that they can be passionate about making the world a better place to inhabit.

Jack and Esther were able to confront what we might call the seductions of black nationalism. For many of us who were coming of age in the 1960s, it was important to know that we could be passionately engaged with the struggle for black liberation, and at the same time fight for the emancipation of the working class and oppressed people throughout the world. Jack taught us these lessons through his political writings and activism. *Freedomways* was palpable evidence of the linkage of black liberation, working class emancipation, and internationalism at the foundation of all freedom aspirations. As a result of the brilliance and perseverance of Esther Cooper Jackson, we have 25 years of this amazing journal of culture and politics. We have a chronicle not only of the movement for black liberation, but of so many aspects of our history which have been purged from the dominant accounts. We read articles from *Freedomways* today and we discover so much that resonates with the current period.

I emphasize the internationalism, which we most urgently need right now. The first article in the *Freedomways Reader* is W.E.B. Du Bois's speech to a gathering of the Southern Negro Youth Congress in Columbia, South Carolina almost exactly sixty years ago – on October 20, 1946. I conclude with this passage:

> There could be no more splendid beckoning to the youth of the twentieth century after the flat failures of late civilization, after the flamboyant establishment of an industrial system which creates poverty and the children of poverty, which are ignorance and disease and crime. After the crazy boasting of a white culture that finally ended in wars which ruined civilization in the whole world, in the midst of Allied people who have yelled about democracy and never practiced it, either in the British Empire or in the American Commonwealth or in South Carolina, here is the chance," he said, "for young women and young men of devotion to lift again the banner of humanity. And to walk toward a civilization which will be free and intelligent, which will be healthy and unafraid, and build in the world a culture led by black folk and joined by people of all colors and all races, without poverty, without ignorance, without disease.

INDEX

Abrahams, Peter 16
Africa, identification with 60
agrarian reform demands 81, 82, 83
Agricultural Adjustment Act 21
Alston, Christopher Columbus 7, 26
American Dilemma project xii, 14, 23
American Youth Congress 27
Americans for Democratic Action 87
Anderson, Carol 5
Anderson, Michael 89-99
Angelo Herndon Case (1932) 21
anti-lynching campaigns 21, 73
Aptheker, Herbert 61

Baker, Ella 36-7, 38
Baldwin, James 62, 65
'Behold the Land': Du Bois 1,
    18-19
Belafonte, Harry 62, 95
Bell, Derek 62
Berger, Victor 75
Bethune, Mary McLeod 51
Binder, Guyora 101-2
Birmingham desegregation of park
    benches 31
    Jacksons in 8-9, 31
    SNYC conference 7, 8
black left feminism *see* feminism
Blum, John Morton 52
Bolshevik Party in Soviet Union 77
Bond, Jean Carey 3, 57, 59-60, 65
Bontemps, Anne 62
Boyd, Herb 70
Brenco, Eliza 92
British colonialism 53, 55
British-American Tobacco
    Company 7, 26
Bronx 'slave market' 36-7
Brooks, Gwendolyn 62

Browder, Earl 41, 83
Brown, Jeanetta Welch 51
Brown, Sarah Hart 5, 12
Brown, Sterling 62, 70
Brown vs. Board of Education 20, 58-9,
    85, 103
Browne, Robert 62-3
Bunche, Ralph xii, 13, 70
Burma, James Jackson in 32, 41, 45,
    46-8, 70
Burnham, Dorothy 6, 45, 60, 66, 105
Burnham, Louis 1, 5-6, 7, 18, 57-8,
    89, 105
    and FEPC 29
    and *Freedom* 57
    and *Freedomways* 61
    and Hansberry 96-7
    photograph 74
Burns, Haywood 62
Burroughs, Margaret 60
buses
    Montgomery boycott 58, 103
    SNYC activism 8-9
Bush, George H.W. 69
Bush, George W. 69, 102

Calloway, Cab xi
Capalbo, Carmen 95
capitalism 19-20
    global 104
Caravan Puppeteers xv, 9
    and Nora Wilson case 27-8
Castro, Fidel 59
Cavalcade arts magazine 9
Childress, Alice 95
churches and civil rights
    movement 87
CIO (Congress of Industrial
    Organizations) 26, 27, 36, 86

and Cold War ideology 88
　Operation Dixie 87
civil liberties cases 21, 23
　Nora Wilson 27-8
Civil Rights Congress 9, 32
civil rights movement
　beginning of 21, 85, 103
　Communist Party in 21
Civil Rights Unionism 85-8
　collapse of 87
Clarke, John Henrik 60
class struggle
　and national oppression 78-9
　and racism 74, 78
colonialism 16, 53, 54, 55
　and US black oppression 52
Combahee River Collective 38
Comintern 77-81, 83
　and CPUSA 80, 81-2
　on Negro Soviet Republic 80
　on self-determination 78, 80-1,
　　82, 83
Communism
　'Death for Negro lynching' 81
　and gender equality 6
　and 'oppressed nation' view
　　78, 80
　see also CPUSA
Communist International 77
Communist Labor Party 77
Communist, The (CPUSA) 80, 81, 83
Connor, 'Bull' xi, 31, 96
Cooke, Marvel 11, 36-7, 38
Cooper, George Posia 12
Cooperative Independent
　Movement 22
CPUSA (Communist Party of the
　USA) ix, xii
　and anti-communism 87
　attorneys 21
　black Americans' view of 22
　in civil rights movement 21
　and Comintern 80, 81-2
　foundation of 77
　intellectual work 6
　and Jacksons' membership 2-3, 9
　political roots 73
　social class of members 11

United Front period 21
Craner, Lawrence 29
Crisis magazine 14, 36, 58
Cuba 59
Current, Gloster 17
Cutler, Addison 34

Dale, Thelma 7, 8, 51
Davis, Angela 1, 38, 62, 65, 66
　on James and Esther Jackson
　　101-6
Davis Jr, Benjamin J. 11, 20
Davis, Ossie 62
Davis, Sallye Bell 7, 8
　photograph 105
Debs, Eugene V. 73-4, 77, 101
Dee, Ruby 62, 65
defense industries, employment in 29
democracy
　current struggle 102-3
　and gender equality 51
Dickinson, Pearl Lee 70
discrimination, examples of x-xi
　see also racism
diversity, use of term 104
Dixon, Frank 28
Dobbs, Malcolm 28
domestic division of labour 6
domestic workers
　Bronx 'slave market' 36-7
　exploitation of 35, 36
　social stigma 35
　strike photograph 37
　see also 'Negro Women Domestic
　　Workers'
Domestic Workers Union 36
Double Victory campaign 50-1, 86
Douglas, Aaron 13
Douglass, Frederick 7, 14, 22, 70
Du Bois, Shirley Graham
　and *Freedomways* 58, 60, 65
　photograph 59
Du Bois, W.E.B. xvii, 14, 67, 70
　'Behold the Land' 1, 18-19
　Color and Democracy 54
　and Esther Jackson 16-17
　and *Freedomways* 58, 59, 60, 61
　ideological position 12, 17-18,

19-20
legacy 103
photograph 59
self-exile to Ghana 19, 72
on slavery 102
SNYC Conference address
    18-19, 106
and Socialist Party 75

Edwards, John 22
Ellison, Ralph 77
exploitation of African-American
    women 35, 36, 37
    present-day 38-9

Fair Employment Practices
    Commission (FEPC) 29-30
fascism 46, 48, 51, 53
Fast, Howard 12, 18, 19, 30
feminism 87
    black left 1, 33-9
    and McCarthyism 88
Fisk University 13, 34
Ford auto plant 9, 32
Foreman, Clark 18
Franklin, John Hope xii
freedom for capitalism 20, 103
Freedom magazine 57, 89
    Hansberry at 89-90, 94-9
Freedomways xvii, 3, 20, 38, 57-67
    ceasing publication 66
    controversies within 65
    cover art 63, 64
    editorial approach 60-1
    ideology 62
    impact of 66-7
    as link between activists 67, 106
    purpose and goals 58, 61
    special issues 62, 66
    sponsored events 66
    and Vietnam war 62, 65
    visual artists 62
    women contributors 65-6
Freedomways Reader 61, 71, 106

gender equality
    and Communism 6
    and democracy 51

in marriage 44-5
and wartime activities 51
Gerstle, Gary 52-3
Giovanni, Nikki 62
global struggle 20
Gore, Dayo 5
Graham, Shirley 11, 19
Guevara, Che 59

Hall, Edwina 22
Hall, Jacquelyn 85
Hall, Wiley 27
Hamilton Slope mine 9
Hammer and Hoe: Kelley 5, 6, 8, 16
Hansberry, Lorraine 62, 89-99
    A Raisin in the Sun 95, 96,
        97-8, 99
    at Montevideo Peace Conference
        91-2
    early life 92-4
    and Louis Burnham 96-7
    marriage 95-6
    photograph 92
    writings 97, 98
Haywood, Harry xi-xii, 82
Hegel, G.W.F. 69
history
    Marx on 73
    rejection of lessons 69
Ho Chi Minh xvi
Holloway, Jonathan 16
Home, Gerald 5
Honey, Michael 5
hooks, bell 38
Hopkins, Vilma 26
Howard University 15-16
Hudson, Hosea xiii, 23, 70
Hughes, Langston 18, 62, 69, 70
Hunton, Alphaeus 11, 60
Hurley, Ruby 17
Hurston, Zora Neale 44

inequality, economic, and racism 74
Inter-American Peace Conference
    91-2
International Labor Defense x
internationalism 53-4, 87, 106
Iraq 102

IWW (Industrial Workers of the
    World) 75

Jackson, Esther Cooper ix, x, 87
    and 'Bull' Connor xi, 31
    career xvii, 23, 32
    danger in investigative work 50-1
    and Du Bois at Manchester
        16-17
    early life 7-8, 13-14
    family 12-13, 23
    and FEPC activities 29-30
    first meeting with James 13-14
    and *Freedomways* 58, 59, 60,
        61, 67
    Freedomways Reader 61
    Kelley interview 6
    Michigan Civil Rights Congress 9
    move to Birmingham 7, 8, 14
    'Negro Women Domestic
        Workers' thesis 1, 8, 33-9
    October 2006 symposium xv
    photographs xvii, 54, 59
    public benches in Birmingham 31
    racism in doctor's office 49
    World Youth Conference
        (London) 54
    and Young Writers and
        Artists 30-1
    see also Negro Women
Jackson, Esther Cooper and James
    daughters 16, 41-2, 43
    and Du Bois 12
    egalitarian relationship 44, 45, 55
    historical assessment 11-20
    history making 1-3, 73
    Jackson Papers 41-55
    legacy 101, 102-4, 106
    marriage 14, 16, 23, 43-6, 55
    Maurice Jackson on 69-72
    relationship between 43-4
    wartime letters 41-55
Jackson, James ix, x
    career xvii, 15-16, 23
    CP membership 22
    on death in war 45
    as Eagle Scout 14-15
    early life 7, 14-15

flight to Detroit 9, 32
    founding SNYC 7
    on infidelity in marriage 46
    interviews with Du Bois
        17-18, 19
    Kelley interview 5-6
    as Ku Klux Klan target xi
    memories of 71-2
    October 2006 symposium xv
    photographs xvi, 10, 15
    Russian hat story 71
    and SNYC 23
    war service 32, 41, 45, 46-8, 70
Jackson, Jesse 62
Jackson, Maurice 3, 69-72
Jagan, Cheddi 62
Johnson, Charles S. 7, 13, 34
Johnson, Col Campbell C. 49
Johnson, George H. 29
Johnson, Lyndon: 'Great Society' 60
Johnson, Mordecai 16
Johnson, Timothy 1, 2, 73-84
Jones, Claudia 38, 87
Jordan, June 62

Kaiser, Ernest 59
Kanuga, Vidya 54
Kelley, Robin xviii, 1, 2, 3, 5-10, 16
Kenyatta, Jomo 16
Killens, John Oliver 61-2, 95
King Jr, Martin Luther xiii, 20, 58,
    62, 87-8
Korstad, Robert 5, 85-8
Ku Klux Klan xi, 81

land reform demands 81, 82, 83
Lawrence, Jacob 62, 64
Leab, Daniel J. ix-xiii, 57-67
League of Young Southerners 28
legacies
    after death 102
    defining 101
    selective 102, 103
Lenin, V.I. 77, 78, 79, 82
Lewis, David Levering 1-3, 11-20,
    103
Lewis, Hylan 57
Lincoln, Abbe 62

Litwack, Leon 14
Logan, Rayford 16
'Long Civil Rights Movement' 85
Lorde, Audre 62
Louisiana, Jacksons in 9, 32
lunch counter sit-ins 59, 98
lynching
    anti-lynching campaigns 21, 73
    Communist slogan against 81
    Socialist Party resolution 75-7
'Lynchsong': Hansberry 90-1

McAdory, Mildred 8
McCarthy era xv, 57, 58, 88
    and feminism 88
    repression of history 6
McDuffie, Erik S. 1, 5, 33-9
McGee, William 90
McKay, Claude 62
McNutt, Paul V. 29
McWhorter, Dianne 5
Makonnen, Ras 16
Malcolm X 65
Mallard, Amy 90
March on Washington Movement 86
marriage: gender relations 44-5
Marshall, Paule 62
Martin, Charles ix-x
Marx, Karl 69, 73
Mayfield, Julian 62, 97
Mazique, Jewell 29
Miller, Sally 75, 77
Myrdal, Gunnar xii, 14, 23, 70

NAACP 18, 19, 51-2, 75, 86
    attitude towards SNYC 23
    Du Bois' report to 17
    membership numbers 85
    and war industries employment 29
Nash, Michael xv-xix, 57-67
Nasonov, N. 82
Nation of Islam 59
National Industrial Recovery Act
    (1933) 36
National Labor Relations Act
    (1935) 36
National Labor Relations Board 86
National Negro Congress 37

nationalism, black 52, 59, 106
    Du Bois on 19
'Negro Women Domestic Workers'
    thesis 1, 8, 33-9
    idea for 34
    methodology 35
Nemiroff, Robert 95-6, 97, 99
neo-liberalism 39
neocolonialism 104
Neruda, Pablo 62
New Deal, Roosevelt's 21, 87
Nkrumah, Kwame 16, 62, 65
Nora Wilson case 27-8
Nyere, Julius 62

O'Dell, Jack 62, 70
Operation Dixie 87
Ovington, Mary White 74-5

Padmore, George 16
Pan African Congress (London)
    16-17
Park, Robert 8, 38
Parks, Rosa 20
    and George Bush 102
patriarchy 36, 44
patriotism 52
Patterson, Frederick 18
Patterson, William L. 103
Payne, Charles 14
Pepper, John 80
Pierce, R.R. 29
Pittman, John 11, 20
Pohl, Constance 65
Poitier, Sidney 95
police brutality 9, 10
poll tax, campaign against 9
Popular Front movements 8, 34, 42
    disintegration of 87
poverty of African-American
    women 38-9
Powell Jr, Adam Clayton 18
present-day struggle 38-9
Price, Arthur 28
prisons 104
    current numbers incarcerated
        103, 104
    military and CIA 104

Prokopec, Joseph 81
proletariat, Blacks as urban xiii
    see also class struggle
puppeteers xv, 9, 27-8

racism 49-50, 81, 82
    in army 46, 48-9
    and class struggle 74, 78
    and Nazi persecution of Jews 87
Raisin in the Sun, A: Hansberry 95,
    96, 97-8, 99
Randolph, A. Philip 79
Reed, John 78-9, 82
Richards, Ann 69
Richards, Johnetta 5, 21-32
Richards, Lloyd 95
Right to Vote Club 9
Riley, Clayton 62
riots: Detroit and Newark 60-1
Roberts, Edith 89
Robeson, Eslanda Goode 44
Robeson, Paul 16, 18, 20, 70, 97
    denial of passport 91, 92
    and *Freedom* 57, 90
    and *Freedomways* 61, 62
    marriage 44
    'We Charge Genocide' petition 103
Rocksborough-Smith, Ian 67
Roosevelt, Eleanor 17
Roosevelt, Franklin
    and FEPC 29
    New Deal 21, 87
Roy, M.N. 79
Russian Revolution: impact in US 77
Rzeszutek, Sara E. xviii, 41-55

SCLC (Southern Christian
    Leadership Conference) 59
Scottsboro Case (1931) x, 21, 82
Scout, James Jackson as 14-15
Seeger, Pete xv
self-determination, African American
    78, 80-1, 82, 83
    and sharecroppers meetings 83-4
Share Cropper's Union 83-4
sharecroppers struggle 21, 82, 83
Sheen, Herbert 44
Singh, Nikhil Pal 52

slavery
    defining 101-2
    marriage and legacy of 44-5
Smethurst, James 58, 66
Smith Act and Jackson 9, 19
SNCC (Student Non-Violent
    Co-ordinating Committee) 59
SNYC (Southern Negro Youth
    Congress) xii-xiii, 6-7, 20
    Achievements 32
    activism 8-9
    agenda xv, 42-3, 103
    and anti-communism 9
    arts and culture 9
    Birmingham 1939 conference 7, 8
    civil liberties cases 27-9
    and civil rights movement 32
    Communism of 18, 42
    demise of xv, 1, 32
    Du Bois' report on 17
    founding of 7, 16, 21, 22-3
    inaugural conference 22, 23
    and Jacksons 21-32, 73
        in wartime 41, 42, 43
    journal art 2, 24, 25
    and Nora Wilson case 27, 28
    photograph of 1942 banquet xvi
    and war industries employment 30
    and World Youth Conference
        17-18
social class: Communist Party
    members 11
Social Security Act (1935) 35
Socialist Party 74, 75
    resolution on lynching 75-7
Southern Conference for Human
    Welfare 18, 87
Soviet Union
    Anti-Fascist Youth Committee
        54-5
    domestic workers 35
    Russian Revolution 77
Stalin, Joseph 78
Stalingrad 55
Steele, Jim 71
Strong, Augusta 6, 45, 65, 66, 105
Strong, Edward 1, 9, 18, 57-8, 105
    in Birmingham 7, 8, 14

gender equality 6
marriage 45
Sullivan, Patricia 5
Summers, Martin 44
Sutton, Percy xv
symposium: October 28, 2006 xv

Tamiment Library xv
gift of papers xv, 5, 101
October 2006 symposium xv,
xviii
Teague, Bob 93
tenant farmers unions 21, 83
Terrell, Mary Church 90
Third World revolutions 59
Third World Women's Alliance 38
Thirteenth Amendment 101-2
Thompson, 'Big Bill' 93
Thompson, Louise 37, 38, 44
Thurman, Wallace 44
Tobacco Stemmers and Laborers
Industrial Union 7, 104
tobacco workers
strike 7, 26
unionization of 7, 16, 23-7, 73,
104
working conditions 23-5
Tobacco Workers International Union
(AFL) 7, 25
Tugwell, Rex xiii

unemployment councils 21
unemployment rate of black
women 39
unionism 85-8
United Front period 21
Urban League 86

veterans, black 49
Vietnam war and *Freedomways* 62, 65
voting rights
rally photograph 74
SNYC activism 9

Walcott, Derek 62
Walker, Alice 62
Walker, Margaret 62
Wallace, Henry 29, 93
'war on terror' 39, 103
Ward, Douglas Turner 95
'We Charge Genocide' petition 103
West, Irene 51
WFDY (World Federation of
Democratic Youth) 54-5
White, Charles 62, 63
White, Walter 17, 18, 51
Wilkerson, Doxey 11
Wilkins, Roy 17, 18, 65
Williamson, Joel 14
Winter, Carl xvii
working class 87, 88
World and Africa, The: Du Bois 19
World War II
effect on black freedom
movement 52, 53
Esther Jackson in 32
internationalist discourse 53-4
Jacksons' letters 41-55
James Jackson in 32, 41, 45, 46-8
racism in army 46, 48-9
war industries employment 29
as war to end racism 53
women's activities 51
World Youth Conference (London)
16, 17-18, 54
Wright, Bruce 62
Wright, Sarah 65-6

Young, Coleman 71
Young Communist League 15, 16
Young Jr, Whitney M. 62
Young, P.B. 21-2
Young Progressives of America 93
Young Writers and Artists,
Association of 23, 30-1

Zahavi, Gerald 5